CANADA
in Pictures

VGS

Eric Braun

Lerner Publications Company

Contents

Lerner Publishing Group realizes that current information and statistics quickly become out of date. To extend the usefulness of the Visual Geography Series, we developed www.vgsbooks.com, a website offering links to up-to-date information, as well as in-depth material, on a wide variety of subjects. All of the websites listed on www.vgsbooks.com have been carefully selected by researchers at Lerner Publishing Group. However, Lerner Publishing Group is not responsible for the accuracy or suitability of the material on any website other than <www.lernerbooks.com>. It is recommended that students using the Internet be supervised by a parent or teacher. Links on www.vgsbooks.com will be regularly reviewed and updated as needed.

Website address: www.lernerbooks.com

Lerner Publications Company
A division of Lerner Publishing Group
241 First Avenue North
Minneapolis, MN 55401 U.S.A.

web enhanced @ www.vgsbooks.com

Braun, Eric, 1971-
    Canada in pictures / by Eric Braun.— Rev. & expanded.
      p. cm. — (Visual geography series)
    Summary: A historical and current look at Canada, discussing the land, the government, the culture, the people, and the economy.
    Includes bibliographical references and index.
    ISBN: 0-8225-4679-5 (lib. bdg. : alk. paper)
    1. Canada—Juvenile literature. 2. Canada—Pictorial works—Juvenile literature. [1. Canada.] I. Title.
II. Series.
F1008.2 .B73 2003
971.064'8—dc21   2002008107

Manufactured in the United States of America
1 2 3 4 5 6 - JR - 08 07 06 05 04 03

INTRODUCTION

Canada is the second-largest nation in the world, after Russia, spreading across the northern half of North America from the Pacific coast to the Atlantic. Because of its size, the land holds great variety, including snowy mountains, dense forests, vast prairies, rugged coastlines, icy tundra, and many rivers and lakes. Canada's greatest asset is its huge holdings of natural resources. The land provides excellent resources for fishing, timber, farming, hydroelectric power, petroleum, and iron ore and other minerals.

The country's people are also varied. They range from the native North Americans, including the Inuit, who inhabited this land early on, to the British and French who later settled it. A wide range of immigrants from all over the world have also made modern Canada their home. Canada is officially a bilingual and multicultural nation.

This ethnic diversity has led to some problems. For decades, French-speaking Canadians in the province of Quebec—who say they feel like second-class citizens—have been fighting for the right to

separate from Canada and form their own nation. In 1995 voters only narrowly defeated a referendum in Quebec on separation, and separatist sentiment is still strong. Aboriginal (native) Canadians have been fighting for fair treatment, including the right to educate their own children and to be given back land they claim was taken from them. The Inuit saw the creation in 1999 of a new territory— Nunavut—as a victory for their people, but many land-rights cases are still being fought by native groups.

The United States lies on the other side of Canada's only shared border. Canada's relationship with its powerful neighbor is a major influence on the country's culture and economy. The United States, because its population is nearly ten times as large and its economic prowess is much greater, has taken a dominant role in the relationship. In many ways, Canada depends on the United States. The United States and Canada are each other's most important trading partners.

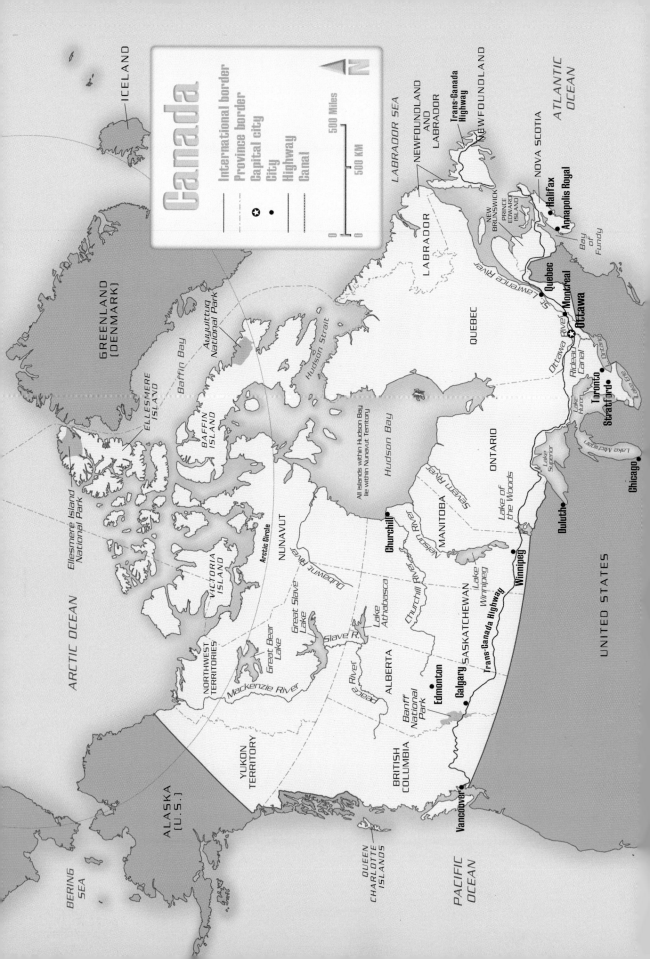

The North American Free Trade Agreement (NAFTA)—implemented in 1992 and involving Canada, the United States, and Mexico—has brought a huge increase in trade for Canada. The economies of the United States and Canada are so tightly tied together that if the U.S. economy falters, so does Canada's.

Most Canadians live within 100 miles (160 kilometers) of the U.S. border, and American culture permeates Canada. But many Canadians take great pride in the ways in which they are un-American. They believe that Canada is kinder and more fair. For example, its universal health-care system is publicly funded, while millions of Americans cannot afford private health care and are left uninsured. Additionally, Canada's public education system is usually perceived to be of higher quality than that of the United States. "We are North Americans," Jean Chrétien, Canada's prime minister, has said, "but not Americans. We have built a different society."

THE LAND

Canada is big—it spans six time zones and covers more than 3.8 million square miles (9.8 million square kilometers). Its territory extends across the upper half of the North American continent, stretching for more than 3,200 miles (5,149 km) from west to east and for 2,875 miles (4,626 km) from north to south.

Canada shares boundaries with only one country—the United States. Part of this frontier snakes through four of the five Great Lakes. To the northwest of Canada is the state of Alaska, and a string of northern U.S. states borders Canada to the south. The large island of Greenland lies within a short distance of Nunavut, a territory in the northwest. Three oceans—the Pacific, the Arctic, and the Atlantic—surround Canada to the west, north, and east, respectively.

◉ Topography

Canada can be roughly divided into six major topographical areas. The small Appalachian region lies in eastern Canada and meets

the St. Lawrence Lowlands farther south. The Canadian Shield resembles a huge, irregular horseshoe with the Hudson Bay in the center. North of the shield is the Arctic Archipelago (a group of islands). The Interior Plains are located west of the Canadian Shield. Farther west, between the Interior Plains and the Pacific Ocean, lies the Cordilleran Region—an area containing several rugged mountain chains.

These landforms stretch across Canada's ten provinces and three territories. The provinces of Newfoundland and Labrador, Nova Scotia, New Brunswick, and Prince Edward Island are located in eastern Canada and are sometimes called the Atlantic Provinces. Quebec and Ontario lie west of Newfoundland. Manitoba, Saskatchewan, and Alberta in south central Canada are known as the Prairie Provinces. British Columbia reaches the Pacific Ocean, making up Canada's western frontier. The Yukon, Northwest, and Nunavut Territories occupy northern Canada.

The rounded peaks of **the Appalachian Region** draw hiking enthusiasts from near and far.

THE APPALACHIAN REGION The Appalachian Region contains the northern extension of a mountain range that crosses the eastern United States. The region includes southeastern Quebec below the St. Lawrence River and most of the Atlantic Provinces. Mount Jacques Cartier is the highest summit in this part of Canada at 4,160 feet (1,268 meters). Erosion has made the mountain system that runs through this area little more than a series of hills.

Some coastal parts of the Appalachian Region—notably the Bay of Fundy—experience high tides. The heavily indented shoreline, where most of the people live, contains excellent harbors for fishing—one of the region's main industries. Most inland areas are gently sloped.

THE ST. LAWRENCE LOWLANDS Lying southwest of Quebec City, the St. Lawrence Lowlands are a series of fertile, low-lying plains bordering the St. Lawrence River and the Great Lakes. Although a small landform, this area is home to about half of the nation's 31 million people. Ease of transportation and excellent links to U.S. ports have encouraged manufacturing and trade in the region. The area's mild climate and rolling countryside make it ideal for farming.

THE CANADIAN SHIELD With an area of nearly 1.6 million square miles (4.1 million sq. km), the Canadian Shield (sometimes called the

Laurentian Plateau) reaches from the Atlantic Ocean to the Arctic Ocean around the Hudson Bay. The region includes large areas of peninsular Newfoundland and Labrador, Quebec, Ontario, Manitoba, Saskatchewan, and the Nunavut Territory.

Marking the western boundary of the shield are Great Bear Lake, Great Slave Lake, Lake Athabasca, Lake Winnipeg, and Lake of the Woods. Along its southern frontier, the shield extends beyond Lake Superior to Lake Huron and borders the St. Lawrence Lowlands and the Appalachian Region to the east.

The Canadian Shield consists mainly of rocky, low-lying terrain that is dotted with thousands of lakes, streams, and swamps. In most places, the shield's elevation reaches less than 1,000 feet (305 m) above sea level. Although the land is unsuitable for farming, it is covered with forests. This region also abounds in minerals and in hydropower (water power) potential. The shield's poor agricultural productivity and harsh climate, however, limit the number of Canadians who live within its boundaries.

Canada holds about two million lakes, covering about 7.6 percent of the nation's landmass. The largest lake entirely in Canada is Great Bear Lake. Located in the Northwest Territories, Great Bear covers 12,100 square miles (31,328 sq. km).

A major shipping destination, the Hudson Bay is one of the largest and most important bodies of water in the Canadian Shield.

A small community on **Baffin Island** nestles at the foot of some low mountains.

THE ARCTIC ARCHIPELAGO North of the Canadian mainland is the Arctic Archipelago, much of which resembles the land in the Canadian Shield. Included in this archipelago are Baffin, Ellesmere, and Victoria Islands. They are, respectively, the fifth, ninth, and tenth largest islands in the world.

Barren and largely unexplored, these islands of the Arctic Circle contain glaciers (moving ice masses) and are marked by fjords (narrow sea inlets). The soil in the region is permanently frozen, but geologists have discovered deposits of petroleum and other valuable minerals beneath the ground.

THE INTERIOR PLAINS West of the Canadian Shield are the Interior Plains, which extend into the Great Plains of the United States. These fertile grasslands cover parts of the Northwest Territories and southeastern British Columbia, but they mostly occupy Alberta, Saskatchewan, and Manitoba. These provinces contain Canada's wheat-growing and cattle-raising regions.

The plains are generally level, although in some places they rise from an elevation of about 800 feet (244 m) to a height of about 2,500 feet (762 m). Many sections are minerally rich, with tar sands (which contain oil), coal, natural gas, lead, and zinc. The northern portions of the Interior Plains are forested and eventually reach barren land in the north called the tundra.

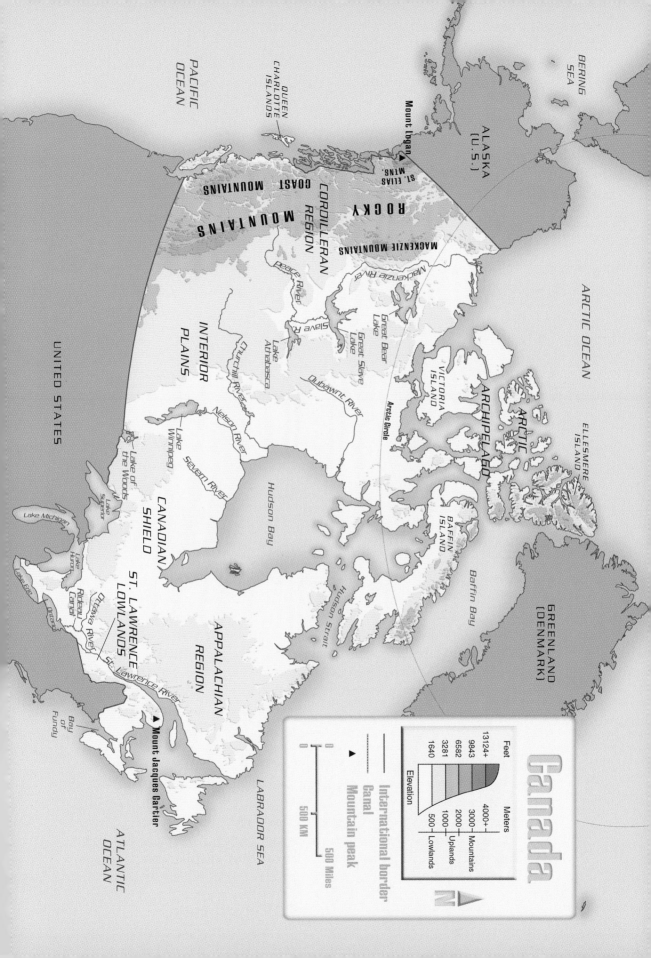

The mighty **Yukon River** cuts a winding path through the peaks and valleys of the Cordilleran Region.

THE CORDILLERAN REGION Rising abruptly from the prairies of western Alberta are the Canadian Rocky Mountains, which mark the beginning of the Cordilleran Region. Extending for roughly 400 miles (644 km) from east to west, the Cordilleran Region includes the Yukon Territory, most of British Columbia, and a small part of southwestern Alberta.

Within the Cordilleran Region lie other mountain ranges. The Coast Mountains—a continuation of the U.S. Cascade Range—stretch northward along Canada's Pacific shore. The St. Elias Mountains rise north of the Coast Mountains along the nation's border with Alaska. A northeastern extension of the Rockies is the Mackenzie Mountains, where tributaries of Canada's two biggest rivers—the Mackenzie and the Yukon—separate from each other to reach the sea. Mount Logan (19,850 feet, 6,050 m) in the St. Elias Mountains is the highest point in

Canada. It is also the second tallest peak in North America, after Alaska's Mount McKinley.

Rivers

Rivers crisscross Canada, making the land fertile and adding to the country's transportation network. Until recently, waterways were the only means of reaching some of Canada's interior regions.

The chief river in eastern Canada is the St. Lawrence, which begins its 760-mile (1,223-km) course in Lake Ontario. The river includes an artificially widened section—called the St. Lawrence Seaway—that links the Great Lakes and the Atlantic Ocean. This connection was built between 1955 and 1959. It allows oceangoing vessels to bring their freight to the city of Toronto in Ontario. Other linkages tie into the seaway, leading to the ports of Chicago and Duluth in the north central United States.

Many rivers flow into the Hudson Bay, an inland sea that covers a total area of 480,000 square miles (1,243,200 sq. km). These waterways include the Churchill, the Nelson, the Dubawnt, and the Severn. At the mouths of these rivers are important ports, such as Churchill and Fort George, which began as trading outposts in the eighteenth century.

With a course of over 2,600 miles (4,183 km), the Mackenzie is Canada's longest river. It collects the waters of the Peace and Slave

British adventurer Alexander Mackenzie began to explore the Mackenzie River in 1789, hoping it would prove to be a quick route to the Pacific Ocean. Modern Canadians use the river for recreation as well as for shipping.

ACID RAIN

In recent decades, Canadians have been concerned about acid rain—precipitation that carries dangerous pollutants such as sulfuric and nitric acids—particularly in the eastern provinces. Smokestacks and cars spew out the pollutants, which bond with oxygen to form toxic acids. Acid rain affects soil fertility, changes the water chemistry of lakes and rivers, and damages vegetation and buildings. Seasonal winds move the pollutants between the United States and Canada. In fact, more than half the acid deposits in eastern Canada originate from emissions in the United States. Canada has enlisted the cooperation of the United States in reducing emissions and fighting acid rain.

Rivers and then makes its way northwestward to empty into Mackenzie Bay. The Yukon begins in the southwestern Yukon Territory and flows for nearly 2,000 miles (3,218 km). The waterway forms part of Canada's border with Alaska, travels across the U.S. state, and empties into the Bering Sea.

◉ Climate

High mountains along Canada's Pacific coast block the warm, moist air that blows in from the Pacific Ocean. The mountains cause the incoming air to rise and to drop rainfall on the coast. These ranges also keep out icy Arctic air during the winter. Vancouver, in the extreme southwest of British Columbia, has average January temperatures above 32°F (0°C). The city's temperatures in July hover between 50 and 68°F (10 and 20°C). Rainfall levels in Vancouver range between 40 and 60 inches (102 and 152 centimeters) per year.

Because the air drops most of its moisture on the Pacific coast, the wind from the west is drier and warmer as it travels eastward. Nevertheless, 15 to 20 inches (38 to 51 cm) of rain fall each year in the prairies of west central Canada. Subzero weather occurs in winter, and summer temperatures average about 66°F (19°C).

In eastern Canada, where most Canadians live, winters are not as severe as they are on the prairies. The Great Lakes, the Atlantic Ocean, and other bodies of water soften temperature extremes in many areas. Toronto, for example, has an average temperature of 25°F (–4°C) in January and 71°F (22°C) in July. The city receives about 30 inches (76 cm) of rain each year. Montréal, Quebec, has somewhat colder winters and more rainfall than Toronto has. Farther east, winters are similar to those in Toronto, but summers are several degrees cooler.

Northern Canada experiences the most severe winters in the country. Summers are brief and fairly warm, and rainfall is heavy in the northeast. In the extreme north, little sunlight occurs during the winter. Average January temperatures hover around –25°F (–32°C), and those in July are below 50°F (10°C).

Flora and Fauna

Forests cover over 1.7 million square miles (4.4 million sq. km) of Canadian territory. The nation's woodlands can be classified into three divisions—northern conifers (evergreens), fir trees, and deciduous (leaf-shedding) trees. The conifers stretch from Newfoundland to the Yukon, and the Pacific coast contains the nation's fir forests. Deciduous trees extend from the Appalachian Region to Lake Huron. About 170 kinds of trees are found in Canada. Among the best known are Douglas fir, hemlock, spruce, birch, maple, and oak.

North of the tree line—beyond which it is too cold for trees to grow—vegetation is composed of grasses and mosses. Flowers in these higher regions bloom only during the brief Arctic summer. The ground underneath, which never thaws, is called permafrost.

Canada's wildlife—once the basis of a thriving fur trade—has played an important role in the nation's economic development. Beaver, mink, muskrat, and other small fur-bearing animals still roam the wilderness, as do bigger game such as moose, deer, bighorn sheep, and bears. The far north is home to seals, walrus, caribou, and polar bears.

Every spring, thousands of ducks and geese migrate to Canada to join many other kinds of birds that make the country their year-round home. Trout, perch, bass, whitefish, and pike thrive in Canada's inland waters. Salmon, halibut, cod, mackerel, haddock, and herring make up part of the nation's saltwater catches.

The frigid climate of Canada's vast northern forests creates a perfect habitat for heavily furred animals, such as the **grizzly bear.** To track the movements of Canadian animals online, go to vgsbooks.com.

The **Ottawa skyline** is a blend of ancient-looking towers and modern office buildings.

Cities

Canada has many urban centers, nearly all of which lie in the southern half of the nation. About 78 percent of all Canadians reside in cities, and most make their homes in the eastern provinces. The capital of Canada is Ottawa, Ontario, but it is not the country's biggest city. That distinction belongs to Toronto, Ontario. Montréal, Quebec, and Vancouver, British Columbia, are Canada's second and third largest cities, respectively.

OTTAWA Located on the southern side of the Ottawa River, Ottawa (metropolitan population 1 million) has been Canada's capital since 1857. Its name comes from *atâwe*—an Ojibwa Indian word that means "to trade." Throughout the 1800s, a British settlement grew on the site after British engineers connected the Ottawa River to Lake Ontario by way of the Rideau Canal.

Rideau Canal

Destroyed by fire in 1900, Ottawa was rebuilt as a manufacturing, governmental, and tourism hub. The city's factories produce communications equipment, paper, furniture, processed food, and chemicals. The federal government, however, employs most of Ottawa's workforce. Visitors travel to the city to enjoy its many parks and public ceremonies. The seasonal events include the Festival of Spring in May and the changing of the guard in front of the Canadian Parliament buildings in the summer months.

TORONTO A busy port on the northeastern shore of Lake Ontario, Toronto has Canada's largest metropolitan population, with 4.3 million people.

The skyscrapers and high-rises of **downtown Toronto** sparkle in the setting sun. Toronto is Canada's largest city.

Founded in 1793 as the capital of the British colony of Upper Canada, Toronto soon prospered. Its name means "meeting place" in the Huron Indian language.

Toronto is Canada's main manufacturing and financial center and produces many of the nation's books and films. The city's industrial sector processes food and makes clothing and wood products. In addition to its manufacturing importance, Toronto contains some of Canada's most famous cultural centers, including the Royal Ontario Museum and the O'Keefe Centre for the Performing Arts.

MONTRÉAL With 3.3 million people, Montréal is the world's second biggest French-speaking city, after Paris. Situated on the banks of the St. Lawrence River, Montréal is Canada's transportation hub. The river links the city to the Atlantic Ocean, and the St. Lawrence Seaway connects it to the Great Lakes. Railways run eastward and westward from the city.

Montréal City Hall sits majestically atop a hill in the heart of Old Montréal. Constructed between 1872 and 1878, City Hall was ravaged by fire in 1922. Miraculously, it remained structurally intact, though the interior and roof were completely destroyed.

Algonquin and Iroquois Indians lived on the site long before Europeans settled there in the seventeenth century. The French established Montréal as part of a small colony, and the British conquered the region in 1760. As a result, the city has a twofold cultural tradition. At times, the differences between the French-descended and the British-descended residents in Montréal have erupted into violence. Some Montréalers support the separation of the French-speaking parts of Canada from the rest of the English-speaking nation.

VANCOUVER Vancouver (population 1.8 million) is the nation's chief port. Bays and straits connect Vancouver to the Pacific Ocean. Warm water currents and the region's mild temperatures prevent the waterways from freezing. As a result, Vancouver's port facilities, unlike those of Montréal and Toronto, are fully usable throughout the year. The moderate weather also attracts large numbers of Canadians looking for a comfortable place to retire.

In the 1960s and 1970s—when trade expanded between North America and Asia—Vancouver's location on the Pacific Ocean increased the city's importance to the nation's economy. Because the city had excellent railway connections to eastern Canada, Vancouver experienced a rise in its national status. Banking and manufacturing expanded in the 1970s and 1980s. The city has become one of the nation's largest financial and industrial centers. Local manufacturing plants take advantage of the region's vast forests to produce paper and wood products. Other plentiful raw materials supply the petroleum and coal industries.

Visit vgsbooks.com for links where you can learn more about Canada's major cities—find out what there is to see and do, get the current weather conditions, see photographs, and more.

SECONDARY CITIES Like the major urban centers, Canada's secondary cities lie mostly in the southern half of Canada. Edmonton (population 863,000), the capital of Alberta, is located in the middle of very productive farmland. The city serves as a crossroads for goods traveling within northwestern Canada.

Calgary (population 822,000) lies in the foothills of the Rocky Mountains. Winnipeg (population 667,000) is the capital of Manitoba, and over half of the province's people live in the city. Quebec City (population 672,000), Canada's oldest urban settlement, lies along the banks of the St. Lawrence River in Quebec province.

The landmark hotel Chateau Frontenac overlooks cafés situated on the St. Lawrence River in Quebec City.

HISTORY AND GOVERNMENT

Perhaps as early as twenty thousand years ago, the earliest inhabitants of what would become Canada crossed a land bridge from Asia to North America. These Asians—whom the Europeans called Indians—arrived in northwestern Canada and gradually migrated eastward and southward. For survival, the newcomers gathered wild food, hunted animals such as wooly mammoth and bison, and fished.

More migrants followed. About five thousand years ago, the earliest ancestors of the Inuit people came to Canada using the same land bridge as the American Indians. (Melting ice later submerged the land bridge, separating Asia from North America.) These people blended with the Thule culture, from which came the direct ancestors of the modern Inuit. After the Inuit arrived in North America, they remained in the Arctic areas of the continent. They hunted whales, seals, caribou, and fish to use for food, clothing, and bone tools. For centuries, the Inuit and the Indians used local resources to feed and shelter themselves.

▷ Early European Explorations

In about A.D. 985, a Norwegian explorer named Erik Thorvaldson (Erik the Red) crossed the sea from Iceland to arrive on the eastern coast of Greenland. There, he encountered Inuit communities and eventually established two settlements. Erik's son, Leif Eriksson, sailed west from Greenland in about 1002, probably reaching Baffin Island and the coast of present-day Newfoundland. Historians regard his explorations as the first landings made by Europeans on the North American continent.

Eriksson eventually returned to Greenland to run the settlements after his father died. By the fourteenth century, lack of funds and harsh climate changes had caused the Norwegian communities in Canada to decline. No further contact occurred between Europe and Canada for many decades.

In the late 1400s, when Europeans renewed their interest in exploration, many distinct Indian cultures thrived in Canada. Some of the largest groupings included the Athapaskan speakers, who dwelt between the Hudson Bay and the western mountains. The Algonquins occupied the northern forests and prairies from the Atlantic to the Rocky Mountains. The Iroquois and the Huron, who were fierce rivals, lived in present-day southern Ontario. The Inuit remained isolated in the Arctic parts of the continent.

Europeans Arrive

John Cabot

In the 1400s, the Europeans were searching for a short route to the luxury goods and wealthy markets of Asia, which the Europeans called the Indies. In 1497 the Italian explorer John Cabot—who was employed by the English king Henry VII—attempted to reach Asia by a northern sea route. Instead, he landed on the eastern coast of Canada, somewhere between Newfoundland and Nova Scotia. He claimed the region for England.

Cabot found neither rich cities nor open markets. He did notice, however, that the offshore waters contained huge amounts of fish, for which Europe was increasing its demand. Soon many English, Portuguese, and French fishers came to the waters off Newfoundland to cast their nets. Eventually, the Europeans realized that these explorations had uncovered a part of the globe they had not previously known. This so-called New World attracted the attention of Europe's kings and queens as a possible source of precious metals.

In 1534 the French king Francis I funded an expedition by Jacques Cartier. Later that year, Cartier found the mouth of the St. Lawrence River and landed on Gaspé Peninsula. In 1535 he sailed up the St.

To claim Canada for King Francis I of France, explorer **Jacques Cartier** planted a cross at Gaspé, near Percé Rock, Quebec, in July 1534.

Lawrence to the Iroquois village of Stadacona and then farther upstream to another Indian village named Hochelaga. (Later, these settlements would be the sites of Quebec City and Montréal, respectively.) Cartier claimed the fertile new land for France, while the Iroquois maintained that it belonged to them.

Europeans originally called the Inuit Eskimos, which means "eaters of raw meat" in the Inuit language. Only in recent years have nonnatives come to call the Inuit the name they prefer. In the Inuit language, Inuit means simply "people."

TRADE DEVELOPMENTS AND ENGLISH INTEREST Though they had no permanent settlements, European fishers continued to take advantage of the region's rich fishing grounds. Docking to dry their fish in the sun, these fishers frequently came in contact with the area's Indians. The Indians wanted to exchange animal furs for the Europeans' fishing equipment.

In time, a brisk fur trade developed, mostly between French fishers and the local inhabitants. The French sent the pelts to France. Sometimes the Indian groups—particularly the Iroquois and the Huron—competed with one another for control of the Indian side of the fur trade.

Meanwhile, England had renewed its interest in exploration. In 1583 Sir Humphrey Gilbert landed in Newfoundland and claimed it for England. Later expeditions traveled to regions farther west. In 1610 the English explorer Henry Hudson tried to find a route to the Indies. His efforts brought him to the huge inland sea that is the present-day Hudson Bay.

French Colonization

With their fur trade increasingly successful, the French viewed their land in the New World as the basis of a French empire. Yet the region was not completely under French control. The French king Henry IV took steps to strengthen his claims to Acadia (parts of present-day Nova Scotia and New Brunswick)—the first French colony in North America. He granted land in the New World to wealthy French people. In return, they took on the job of colonizing the area. In 1605 Samuel de Champlain founded a permanent settlement at Port Royal (later Annapolis Royal, Nova Scotia).

In 1608 Champlain established Quebec City at a strategic point on the St. Lawrence River to gain control of the fur trade of the St. Lawrence Valley. Champlain developed Quebec City's fur trade and brought colonists to the region that was called New France. In 1615 French

Samuel de Champlain went on his first voyage to Canada in 1603 on a fur-trading expedition. It wasn't until his second trip that he began exploring the area and creating colonies for France. During his time in Canada, he explored from the Bay of Fundy down to Cape Cod in the United States.

missionaries arrived to convert the Indians to Christianity. Over the next thirty years, many more missionaries landed in search of converts.

European immigration into Indian regions disrupted local cultures. Foreign diseases, such as smallpox, caused many deaths among the Indians. Europeans claimed Indian hunting lands, a move that restricted the ability of the inhabitants to find food and to practice their traditional way of life. Competition over the fur trade worsened rivalries that already existed among various Indian groups.

The 1600s

In the seventeenth century, attacks by the British and the Iroquois discouraged Europeans from settling in New France. In 1627 the French government organized the Company of the Hundred Associates to carry on trade with the New World. The company was required to increase New France's population by three hundred colonists each year. This goal was small compared to the large number of British and Dutch settlers who had taken over territories and had set up colonies south of New France (part of the modern United States).

In 1627—when a war broke out in Europe between Britain and France—the British attacked French-held land in North America. By 1629

When French explorers and traders first came to Canada in the 1600s, many of them married native women, especially Cree women. Their children were called Métis, which means "mixed" in French. The name Métis is still used to describe Canadians of mixed native and white heritages.

Quebec City had fallen into British hands. The settlement was returned to France in 1632, following a treaty between the warring parties. The status of New France, however, remained uncertain.

Because of the explorations of Henry Hudson, the British claimed the same part of eastern Canada that the French held. Furthermore, the French were clashing with the Iroquois. These Indians wanted to divert the fur trade to the south, where they could exchange pelts for Dutch firearms and other goods. By 1651—after destroying their Indian competitors—the Iroquois were dominating the Indian side of the fur trade.

In 1663, to stop the Iroquois and to encourage colonization, the French king Louis XIV sent troops to New France. Constant fighting forced some of the Iroquois to sign peace treaties. By 1679 almost ten thousand people were living in New France, and fur trading remained the region's main industry.

British-French Conflict

In the late seventeenth century, the traders of New France found themselves in conflict with the merchants of the British colonies farther south. These two groups disagreed about who should control the fur trade. They also argued about ownership of the area around the Hudson Bay, which both France and Britain claimed.

In 1670 the British king Charles II granted a royal charter to a commercial firm called the Hudson's Bay Company. The company established outposts and forts along the shores of the Hudson Bay. Because it had many outlets, the Hudson's Bay Company attracted Indian and colonial customers and threatened to cut off an important source of French income. France responded by attacking some of the outposts, and Britain retaliated. For several decades, clashes continued, and relations between the two European powers remained tense.

Trade posts run by the **Hudson's Bay Company** quickly became an important part of the early Canadian economy.

From 1702 to 1713, the British and French fought each other in the New World in Queen Anne's War. In 1713 the warring parties ended the conflict by signing the Treaty of Utrecht. This document forced France to recognize British claims to the Hudson Bay, Acadia (renamed Nova Scotia), and Newfoundland.

FRANCE'S FINAL DEFEAT As a result of these land gains, British traders and pioneers began moving into French territory. These movements worsened tensions between France and Britain. In 1753 clashes erupted in North America, and in 1756 the fighting spread to Europe.

The fighting pitted the British, their colonial subjects, and their Indian allies against the French and their Indian supporters. The British, who were more numerous, wanted the French to leave North America. The British took Quebec City in 1759 and conquered Montréal in 1760. The Treaty of Paris, signed in 1763, gave all of France's territories in what later became Canada to the British.

British Rule

The British named their newly acquired territory Quebec. They governed it under British laws, which discriminated against the French in the colony. For example, under British law, no member of the Roman Catholic religion could hold public office. Most of the French settlers belonged to this faith, while the British did not.

Quebec's early governors saw that this arrangement would not encourage colonial loyalty—a problem the British government was also having with its thirteen colonies to the south (the present-day eastern United States). Encouraged by the governors, the British Parliament changed the laws that ruled Quebec. In 1774 it passed the Quebec Act, which gave the French population religious liberty and the right to follow their own laws.

UPPER AND LOWER CANADA Many British colonists remained loyal to Great Britain during the American Revolutionary War, which began in 1775. During and after the conflict, thousands of settlers fled northward to Nova Scotia and Quebec. These newcomers were called loyalists. Soon, the loyalists in Nova Scotia wanted their own colony, and in 1784 New Brunswick was formed from some of Nova Scotia's land.

Conflicts continued between the British and the French colonists, principally about their differing religions and laws. In 1791 the British Parliament passed another act. This decree divided Quebec into two colonies—British-dominated Upper Canada and French-dominated Lower Canada.

In 1784, after the American Revolutionary War ended, **the first loyalists** settled at the present site of St. John, New Brunswick.

Upper Canada covered part of the Great Lakes region and the upper St. Lawrence River. Lower Canada consisted of areas along the lower reaches of the St. Lawrence River. Each of the newly formed colonies had an elected assembly, but the British still governed all colonial territories.

EXPANSION CONTINUES The Revolutionary War did more than create the United States of America. British traders lost important areas of commercial exchange, and Indian groups moved westward to escape British and U.S. expansion. As a result, the fur trade broadened its scope, seeking more pelt sources and establishing outposts farther and farther west. New areas of British North America (as Britain's entire holdings were called) were explored.

European westward expansion in the 1800s began a period during which the Indians of North America lost much of their land. As Europeans "discovered" more of the continent, settlement soon followed. In the populated east, the number of Indians dwindled, as Europeans relocated them to specific pieces of land called reserves (land set aside for aboriginals). The huge herds of buffalo—a primary source of meat for many Indian groups of the prairies—were slowly shrinking because of westward European settlement. This loss affected the hunting lifestyles of the Indians.

Development and Reform

During the first half of the nineteenth century, Upper and Lower Canada continued to develop. New roads and canals improved communications, and more farmland came under the plow.

As the population increased and as commerce grew, so did discontent with the colony's form of government. Power was concentrated in the hands of a small number of influential British people. French Canadians, who owned few businesses, felt that their culture and way of life were threatened by the thousands of English-speakers who arrived in the early 1800s. British Canadians favored policies that helped to increase trade and that benefited business more than agriculture.

Demands for political reform sparked two rebellions in 1837. Louis Joseph Papineau, a politician in Lower Canada, led one revolt, and William Lyon Mackenzie in Upper Canada headed the other. British and colonial troops put down the rebellions, which both lasted only a short time. The leaders and supporters of the movements fled to the United States.

In 1838, as a result of the revolts, the British Parliament sent John Lambton, earl of Durham, to investigate political conditions in Canada. Lord Durham suggested that British North America be granted more self-government. Although the British cabinet rejected this reform, it did agree to another of Durham's suggestions—that Upper and Lower Canada be united. The Act of Union was in place by 1841. The combined territory was called the Province of Canada.

In the 1840s, the provinces of British North America—which by then included Canada and the Atlantic Provinces of Prince Edward Island, Nova Scotia, and New Brunswick—sought "responsible government" (control over local affairs). By 1850 Britain had granted most of the provinces a style of administration that gave them some regional authority.

British North America developed alongside its neighbor, the United States. Trade and transportation links opened between the two regions. British North America used these opportunities to expand its economy, which included textile manufacturing, fishing, logging, and flour milling.

Louis Joseph Papineau led one of two rebellions that took place in Canada in 1837.

After the American Civil War ended in 1865, the United States sought to increase its commercial power. Without a large army, Canadians began to fear U.S. domination of North America. These concerns were among many ideas that made a federation of provinces attractive to Canada.

The Dominion of Canada

Representatives of Canada and the Atlantic Provinces met to work out the details of a federation among themselves. They presented the plan to the British government in 1866, and Parliament passed the British North America Act in 1867. The act formed the Dominion of Canada, which had a parliamentary system with an elected house of commons and an appointed senate. A governor-general represented the British monarch, who continued to be head of state. Although more self-governing, Canada was still not a fully independent nation.

The act brought together the provinces of Ontario (once called Upper Canada), Quebec (formerly Lower Canada), Nova Scotia, and New Brunswick. Newfoundland and Prince Edward Island refused to join. John A. Macdonald, leader of Canada's Conservative Party, became the first prime minister of the Dominion of Canada.

John A. Macdonald

Slowly, other provinces and areas were brought into the new confederation. The Canadian government purchased the vast holdings of the Hudson's Bay Company in 1870. The Northwest Territories and the province of Manitoba were created from these lands. British Columbia joined Canada in 1871 after it was promised a railway link with the east (completed in 1885). Prince Edward Island entered the confederation in 1873.

EARLY CHALLENGES A scandal over political contributions and railway contracts toppled the Macdonald government in 1873. Alexander Mackenzie, head of the Liberal Party that won the elections that followed, became the dominion's prime minister. His administration made improvements that gave Canadians greater authority over their own affairs. Mackenzie, however, could not halt the effects of an economic slump, and another Macdonald administration replaced the Liberal government in 1878.

High on Macdonald's agenda was completion of the coast-to-coast railway that had earlier caused his resignation. The near completion of the track sparked rebellions in the late 1870s and 1880s among the Métis—a group of farmers who were of both French and Indian ancestry.

Louis Riel

(They had also revolted during Macdonald's first government.) The Métis feared the loss of their farmlands as the railway brought more settlers to central Canada. In 1885 Louis Riel led the North West Rebellion of Métis against the Canadian government. The revolt was again swiftly crushed, and Riel was executed for treason.

⊙ Economic Growth

By the end of the nineteenth century, Canada had begun to show its economic potential. Agriculture, mining, forestry, fishing, and manufacturing increased. The Canadian Pacific Railway began providing passenger service in 1886, and huge numbers of settlers and immigrants traveled westward. Some arrived to farm the prairies. Others were attracted by the discovery of gold in the Klondike area of the Northwest Territories.

In 1898 a new region—the Yukon Territory—was formed around the Klondike. In addition, so many people had settled in the prairies that the government of Wilfred Laurier—Canada's first French Canadian prime minister—created two new prairie provinces to go with Manitoba. Alberta and Saskatchewan were added to the Dominion of Canada in 1905.

In the first decade of the twentieth century, Canada welcomed thousands of immigrants. The population leapt from 5.4 million in 1901 to 7.2 million in 1911. Much of the increase resulted from

Mounted police kept order during **Canada's first gold rush** in 1898.

discoveries of precious metals that lured prospectors to British Columbia and the Yukon Territory.

World War I and Independence

Under Robert L. Borden, a Conservative prime minister who came to power in 1911, Canada allied itself with Britain against Germany in World War I (1914–1918). Over 600,000 Canadians served in Canadian regiments, and 63,000 died in battle. The Borden administration had promised not to draft young Canadians to fight overseas. By 1917, however, the government could not fill its quotas with volunteers and began a nationwide draft. This issue divided the English-speaking Canadians—who supported the draft—from the French Canadians, who opposed it. A Conservative-Liberal coalition government emerged in 1917, again headed by Borden.

Canada made substantial amounts of money during the war by manufacturing ships and weapons and by supplying food. Because of its military participation in the global conflict, Canada demanded greater freedom in making its own foreign and defense policies. These matters had been in the hands of politicians in Great Britain. Britain realized how much it depended on colonial labor and resources for its own survival. As a result, it granted Canada's demands for more self-government, without giving the dominion complete independence.

In 1921 William Lyon Mackenzie King, head of the Liberal Party, became prime minister. One of his main goals was to secure Canada's independence from Great Britain. He met with British leaders in 1926 and again in 1930 to confirm Canada's status as an independent nation and to hammer out the details of the Statute of Westminster. Passed by the British Parliament in 1931, this act established Canada's independence in both internal and external affairs. The Canadian provinces also wielded considerable local power. The British monarch remained the symbolic head of state.

EXPLOSION IN HALIFAX

During World War I, naval ships from many countries stopped in the harbor at Halifax, Nova Scotia, to pick up troops and supplies. On December 6, 1917, two ships collided in the fog there. One of the boats was the *Mont Blanc*, a French ship carrying explosives. Both ships went up in flames. The massive explosion killed two thousand people and injured another eight thousand, as well as leveling much of the town of Halifax. Over many years, the city was rebuilt. Residents of Halifax gather every December 6 in a park overlooking the harbor to remember the people who died and the people who helped rebuild the city.

William Lyon Mackenzie King was Canada's tenth prime minister and served from 1921 to 1948. Besides securing Canada's political independence from Great Britain, he also created an old-age pension plan and appointed Canada's first female senator.

The great worldwide economic depression of the 1930s severely affected Canadian prosperity, particularly in the three Prairie Provinces. Canada's foreign trade declined dramatically, grain prices were low, and unemployment was high. The outbreak of World War II in 1939 eased many of Canada's economic woes. Demands increased for textiles, iron, and food. Factories reopened and rehired workers to meet the new wartime quotas.

World War II and Its Aftermath

Canada joined the anti-German alliance on the side of Great Britain during the Second World War. The nation did not, however, draft soldiers or supply troops. By late 1941, Canada had also allied itself with Britain and the United States against Japan. Eventually, more than one million Canadian men and women joined the armed forces, participating in battles in Asia and Europe. Over 90,000 were killed or wounded in the global conflict.

When the war ended in 1945, Canada turned its attention to internal reforms. Huge numbers of immigrants arrived from war-damaged countries in Europe and Asia. The newcomers swelled the urban populations, causing suburbs to multiply. The construction industry thrived as it tried to keep up with housing demands.

The King administration wanted to ensure the well-being of all Canadians. It enacted a broad range of social programs that included unemployment insurance, good veterans' benefits, better pensions for senior citizens, and improved health care. These programs helped to give ordinary Canadians a high standard of living. As a sign of its approval of Canada's prosperity, Newfoundland and Labrador voted to become Canada's tenth province in 1949.

Under King's successor, Louis St. Laurent, the country became actively involved in international affairs. Canada was a founding member of the United Nations (UN). In 1949 the nation signed a defense treaty—called the North Atlantic Treaty Organization (NATO)—with the United States and countries in Western Europe. Canada's new role in foreign affairs involved the country in the Korean War (1950–1953) and in Middle Eastern conflicts in the 1950s. The nation often supplied peacekeeping forces during international disputes.

The Separatist Movement

While Canada was strengthening its international role, an age-old challenge reappeared within the nation. People in Quebec—the home of most of Canada's French Canadians—again voiced their resentment at being a minority population. The idea of separating Quebec from the rest of Canada took root. Activists founded separatist groups, including a terrorist organization called the Front de Libération du Québec (FLQ). A new political party, the Parti Québécois (PQ), championed the separatist cause in Quebec's legislature.

In 1968 a French Canadian from Quebec, Pierre Trudeau, became prime minister as head of the winning Liberal Party. One of his goals was to settle the separatist issue. Trudeau won the Canadian Parliament's approval of the Official Languages Act. This legislation gave the French language equal status with English in the government. By nationally recognizing Canada's French heritage, Trudeau hoped to unify the country. But the act had little effect.

During his time in office, **Pierre Trudeau** *(center)* tried to pacify French Canadian separatist groups. Here, he leaves the Canadian Parliament after discussing an FLQ bombing that had killed a Canadian senator.

The PQ won a majority of seats in Quebec's legislature in 1976. The party's leader, René Levesque, became provincial prime minister. His administration held a vote in Quebec on the separatist issue. About 60 percent of Quebec's voters rejected a proposal that would have empowered leaders of the province to negotiate for Quebec's independence.

Under a new government in 1980, Trudeau tried to foster greater Canadian unity. He also sought to weaken the country's ties to Great Britain. This goal resulted in the Constitution Act of 1982, which eliminated Britain's role in Canada's constitutional life.

The Canadian economy worsened in the 1980s, as unemployment rose to its highest rate since the depression of the 1930s. Trudeau resigned in 1984, and the Progressive Conservative Party (PCP) won the subsequent general election. Brian Mulroney, also from Quebec, became Canada's prime minister.

Brian Mulroney

By resolving longstanding economic disagreements—about oil rights in the west and fishing rights in the east—Mulroney addressed some of Canada's financial problems. His most ambitious international proposals, however, were the 1988 Free Trade Agreement (FTA) with the United States and the 1992 North American Free Trade Agreement (NAFTA) with the United States and Mexico. Under the provisions of these documents, no import taxes are charged on most goods exchanged among the three nations.

Still, during the early 1990s, Canadians lost more than 400,000 manufacturing jobs, and the overall unemployment rate grew steadily. Facing growing opposition to his economic policies, Mulroney stepped down from his post as prime minister in June 1993. He was replaced by his party's Kim Campbell, who became Canada's first woman prime minister.

◉ The Chrétien Era

Campbell was unable to restore the nation's faith in the PCP, and in the general elections in November 1993, the party suffered a decisive defeat. The Liberal Party, led by Jean Chrétien, came out with a clear majority, and Chrétien succeeded as prime minister. The new Liberal government worked to improve the nation's economy by significantly reducing defense spending and implementing an elaborate job creation scheme.

Jean Chrétien

By this time, several groups of Canada's aboriginal peoples (the collective name for Indians and Inuit) had begun to dispute the government's right to lands the aboriginals claimed had been unfairly taken from them. In Quebec armed confrontations took place between authorities and militant aboriginal groups.

In 1993 the federal government agreed to establish the Nunavut Territory out of a section of the Northwest Territories. Nunavut—which would be self-governing but still a part of Canada—would come into existence in April of 1999. The population already living in the area that would become Nunavut was 85 percent Inuit, and the Inuit celebrated the promise of this vast, semi-autonomous territory as a victory for Inuit rights.

Another group seeking autonomy, the separatists of Quebec, raised the issue of secession for Quebec again in 1995. Once again, a referendum on secession was held, and this time it was defeated by only a 1 percent margin. In 1998 the Supreme Court ruled that if Quebec (or any province) voted to secede, it could only carry out the action with the federal government's consent. Furthermore, the measure would have to be approved by the governments of at least seven of the ten provinces.

On April 1, 1999, as promised, the territory of Nunavut was formed in the northern part of the country. It was the first territory in Canada to have a majority indigenous population. Yet many aboriginal groups are still haggling over land claims in court. For example, after about a decade of unsuccessful negotiations between aboriginal groups and the government over land rights on Canada's north Pacific coast, the Haida Indians brought their case to court in 2002. The Haida have lived

LANDRY VS. THE FEDS

The Quebec separatist movement had seemed slightly quieter after the 1995 referendum was defeated. It got a boost in 2001, when Bernard Landry, founder of the Parti Québécois, was elected as the prime minister of Quebec. Landry vowed to try to achieve independence for the French-speaking province. Since his installation as prime minister, he has clashed with federal leaders many times. He was particularly critical of Prime Minister Chrétien for the federal government's advertising campaign in Quebec supporting national unity. However, it is believed Landry will only call for another referendum if he believes he has the votes to win it.

on the Queen Charlotte Islands for thousands of years and have never signed a treaty with any government. Many believe they have a strong case. They are expected to win rights to all of the islands, an area rich in natural resources.

> To find a variety of resources on the Canadian government—including additional information on the Canadian prime minister, up-to-date headlines on policies and news, and more—go to vgsbooks.com.

Government

The British North America Act of 1867 and the Constitution Act of 1982 are the basis of Canada's governmental framework. Canada is a federation of provinces, with certain powers belonging to the national government and with others left to the provinces. These provincial governments have considerable authority. A cabinet, headed by a prime minister, runs the various departments at the federal level. According to the constitution, the monarch of Great Britain, who is represented by a governor-general, is the head of state. The monarch's role, however, is mainly symbolic.

Canada's two-house parliament has the power to make laws in areas of federal responsibility. This legislative body consists of an elected House of Commons and an appointed Senate. The population of each province determines the number of seats in the house. In general, the leader of the party that wins the greatest number of seats becomes prime minister and selects a

Centre Block, the main building of Parliament, houses Canada's House of Commons and Senate. The distinctive Peace Tower stands at the center of the building.

cabinet from among fellow party members. With the advice of the prime minister, the governor-general appoints Canada's 104 senators.

The nation's court system includes a supreme and a federal court, as well as provincial tribunals. Instructed by the prime minister, the governor-general names the judges on these courts. The Supreme Court, with nine judges on its panel, is the highest court of appeal in both civil and criminal cases. The Federal Court hears both trial and appeal cases. Provincial tribunals enforce national and local laws.

Canada's ten provinces have similar governmental frameworks. The leader of the majority party in the provincial legislature becomes the premier (or in Quebec, the prime minister) of the province. An elected unicameral (one-house) legislature makes laws that govern issues of local concern. The nation's three territories have less powerful administrations, which handle matters involving education, health, and law enforcement.

THE PEOPLE

Canada had a population of more than 31 million people in 2001. The national population density is 8 persons per square mile (3 per sq. km), but this figure can be misleading. About 75 percent of all Canadians live in southern Canada, within 100 miles (160 km) of the U.S. border. In the Yukon, Northwest, and Nunavut Territories—which cover one-third of Canada's area—the total population numbers only 99,000 inhabitants. The population density in this region is about 6.8 persons in every 100 square miles (2.7 people per 100 sq. km). In Ontario, the average ratio is 28.8 Canadians per square mile (11.1 per sq. km). About 78 percent of all Canadians live in cities.

Between 1996 and 2001, Canada's population increased by about 4 percent. During this period, immigration accounted for more than half of the increase—the first time immigration outpaced natural population growth since World War II. A primary reason is that Canadians are living longer (they have a life expectancy of 79 years). The aging population has led to the slowing of fertility rates (11 births per 1,000

people) and rising of the death rate (8 deaths per 1,000 people). Immigration, meanwhile, remains steady.

Ethnic Mixture

Two large and several smaller groups make up Canada's population. The largest group of people, about 28 percent of Canadians, are those who claim British ancestry. Another 23 percent have a French background. Most French Canadians live in the province of Quebec, but the rest of the nation also has areas where the population is largely French. British Canadians are predominant in every province except Quebec.

Since the early 1900s, many other nationalities have found homes in Canada. For most of the twentieth century, the majority of newcomers were from Europe (especially Britain, Italy, Poland, Ukraine, Germany, and the Netherlands) and the United States. About 15 percent of Canadians claim other European backgrounds besides British or French. Approximately 26 percent of Canadians are of mixed descent.

The population of Canada includes immigrants from many countries. Recently, many Asians—such as this **young woman from India** dancing at a local festival on Prince Edward Island—have made the country their home.

In recent years, more people have immigrated to Canada from China, India, the Philippines, and other Asian countries than from anywhere else in the world. Arab and African populations have also been growing. Asians, Arabs, and Africans together make up about 6 percent of Canada's population. These smaller communities—Europeans, Asians, Arabs, and Africans—retain strong ties to their ethnic backgrounds, celebrating traditional holidays and festivals, and have greatly influenced the ethnic makeup of Canada.

The remaining 2 percent of the population consists of Indian and Inuit groups. About half the Indian peoples live on the roughly 2,500 reserves that the Canadian government has established. Many groups—including the Algonquins, the Cree, the Iroquois, and the Sioux—have survived policies that relocated and discriminated against them. In recent years, some Indians have demanded better land and more protection for their distinct cultures. Reserves have become the subject of Indian land claims. The Assembly of First Nations seeks to

PRESERVING INUKTITUT

Until recently, Inuit children were forced to speak English in school and were forbidden to speak their own language, called Inuktitut. After decades of this education, Inuktitut seemed in danger of dying out. Only the elders spoke the native tongue. In modern Nunavut, young people are taught Inuktitut in Inuit schools. The Inuit have worked hard to preserve their native tongue and keep it relevant by inventing words for many modern things, such as computer, fax, satellite, telephone, HIV, Internet, and hockey.

speak for all Indian (or First Nations) people in Canada, and increasingly its voice is being heard.

Inuit man

The Inuit dwell in cold areas of Ontario, Newfoundland and Labrador, Quebec, and the territories. With a strong sense of community, the Inuit are an important part of Canada's ethnic mixture. Traditionally, the Inuit depended on the resources of the sea. But because of efforts to integrate this group into Canada's larger society, many Inuit have ties to both a traditional and a new culture. No longer nomadic, almost all Inuit live in villages, have televisions and telephones, and enjoy most of the amenities of modern life.

STRAINED RELATIONSHIPS Tensions remain between the French- and British-descended groups. Many French-speakers feel that they are discriminated against on economic and social levels because of their language and culture. Even in Quebec, most businesses are owned by English-speakers.

In addition to the French-British dilemma, Canada's unity suffers from an east-west hostility. People from British Columbia, for example, have felt that their natural resources have been unfairly exploited by the national government in Ottawa. Even within individual

A man in Montréal waves the flag of Quebec. The national Canadian government continues to struggle with French Canadians' desire for independence.

Canadian provinces, antagonism exists. Alberta's Calgarians and Edmontonians, for instance, are strong rivals.

Compounding these internal struggles is Canada's complex and sometimes strained relationship with the United States. Films, books, television shows, and magazines from the United States flood the Canadian market. U.S. firms own many businesses throughout Canada. In addition, many Canadians leave Canada to live and work in the United States, where wages are higher and taxes are lower, leading to fears of a Canadian "brain drain." At times, strong anti-Americanism has arisen among Canadians who feel that their powerful southern neighbor threatens Canada's separate lifestyle.

Education

Education is free and compulsory for all Canadian children. Canada has a largely literate population. About 99 percent of those older than fifteen have at least a ninth-grade education. The governments of the provinces and territories regulate Canada's school systems, which differ from

province to province or territory. The federal government is responsible for the education of the Indians and the Inuit, the armed forces personnel and their dependents, and inmates of federal correctional facilities. However, many aboriginal groups have taken political action in an attempt to gain control of their educational systems. They prefer locally controlled schools that reflect their own languages and cultures.

Depending on which province or territory Canadian children live in, they are required to attend school from the age of six or seven until they are fifteen or sixteen. Students may attend public or private schools, and in some provinces they may attend public "separate" schools, established and run by religious groups. All nonprivate education through secondary (high) school is publicly funded.

Elementary schools focus on language, math, social studies, introductory arts, and science. Secondary schools have two tracks. The first prepares students for attending a university, and the second prepares them for postsecondary education at a community college or institute of technology, or for the workplace.

Elementary school boys in Vancouver study math.

A growing number of Canadian young people are entering the nation's colleges and universities. Canada has about one hundred universities and two hundred technical institutes and community colleges. About one million Canadians attend postsecondary schools, which are funded largely by government subsidies. English-language universities are patterned primarily after those in the United States. French-language universities have some similarities with French schools. The largest Canadian institution to offer bilingual (two-language) instruction is the University of Ottawa in Ontario.

> If you'd like to find out more about Canadian people, including indigenous groups like the Inuit, go to vgsbooks.com, where you'll find links to websites that have photographs and additional information on Canada's diverse population.

⊙ Health

Since the 1960s, a publicly funded national health care system has provided high-quality care at little cost to patients. As a result, Canadians in general have a standard of health that is among the best in the world. For example, Canada has a lower infant mortality rate and a higher life expectancy than the United States does. Only 5.5 Canadian babies die out of each 1,000 live births (compared to 7.1 for the United States).

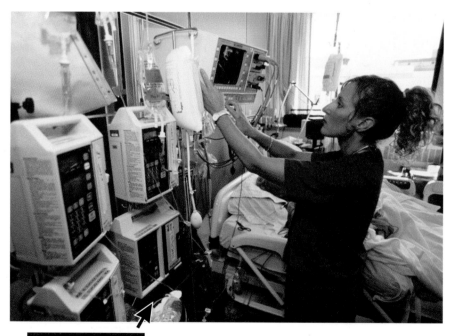

An **intensive care nurse** checks a patient's monitor at Lion's Gate Hospital in Vancouver. High quality health care is available to all Canadian citizens.

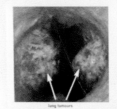

WARNING:
CIGARETTES CAUSE LUNG CANCER

85% of lung cancers are caused by smoking. 80% of lung cancer victims die within 3 years.

Health Canada

lung tumours

Cigarettes

The average Canadian can expect to live to age 79, the third-highest life expectancy in the world, behind only Switzerland and Japan.

However, good health is not shared equally by all Canadians. Age, gender, education, and income level influence health statistics in a number of important ways. Most notably, individuals with low incomes are more likely to suffer illnesses and to die early than those with higher incomes. Also important, Canada's aboriginal peoples are at a much higher risk for poor health and early death than the Canadian population as a whole. The prevalence of all major chronic diseases, including diabetes, heart problems, and cancer, is significantly higher in aboriginal communities. The average income of an aboriginal person is about one-half that of a nonnative Canadian.

Sadly, suicide is an important contributor to Canada's death rate, especially among young people. Canada's rate of youth suicide (suicide by individuals aged 15 to 24) is one of the world's highest. Suicide among aboriginal groups in Canada has been reported to be two to seven times more frequent than in the Canadian population at large.

SMOKING

In Canada, smoking is a leading cause of early death, far outweighing suicide, motor vehicle crashes, AIDS, and murder combined. Smoking is estimated to be responsible for at least 25 percent of all deaths for adults between the ages of 35 and 84. In response, the Canadian government started putting graphic warning labels on cigarette packages *(above)* in 2001. The full-color photographs cover half of the front and back of each package of cigarettes. They depict a diseased mouth, a lung tumor, a brain after a stroke, a damaged heart, and a limp cigarette that warns of impotence. A majority of smokers interviewed—58 percent—said the pictures made them think more about the health effects of smoking. The warnings were so effective that 44 percent of the smokers polled said the warnings increased their motivation to quit smoking.

CULTURAL LIFE

From the time of colonization through well into the twentieth century, the majority of Canada's population was British, and its culture generally reflected a British point of view. Even after the Statute of Westminster was passed in 1931 establishing Canada's independence from Britain, the country maintained a distinctly British identity. But as the twentieth century progressed and as immigrants began to make up more and more of Canada's population, the personality of the nation began to change. In 1965 Canada replaced the British flag with the maple leaf—a sure sign that the British identity was weakening—and in 1971 the federal government declared that Canada was officially a multicultural nation. Peoples who were once immigrants or descendants of immigrants began to have a say in political affairs. They also had a means to preserve their cultures within the fabric of Canadian society.

Canadian culture is also greatly influenced by the country's neighbor to the south, the United States. American culture—in books,

in magazines, on radio, on television, and in movies—is pervasive. Even American speech patterns have an increasing influence on the English spoken in Canada. Many Canadians feel a closer bond with their American neighbors just across the border than they do with fellow citizens who may live thousands of miles away.

Language

Canada is officially a bilingual country. The Official Languages Act of 1969 gives all Canadians the right to communicate with the federal government in either French or English. About 67 percent of the population speaks English only, and about 14 percent speaks French only. Another 17 percent speaks both.

Most French-speaking people live in Quebec, where French is the official language of the province. Quebec's French-speaking citizens are called Québécois. The French spoken by Québécois is distinct from the French used in France. It has absorbed and redefined some

Every June 24, people in Quebec celebrate their pride in being from Quebec by marking **Saint Jean Baptiste Day**, a provincial holiday. A big parade in Montréal is followed by a televised outdoor concert and fireworks. People fly Quebec's flag and have picnics and other festivities.

English words. Joual—the urban Québécois slang—contains local expressions that use a unique style of pronunciation.

English, too, has undergone variations that distinguish the forms spoken in Canada from the European tongue. People from Newfoundland, for example, speak a thickly accented English dialect, with faint Irish overtones. Many of the local sayings are difficult for outsiders to understand.

About 16 percent of Canadians identify languages other than French or English as their primary language, but only about 2 percent of Canadians cannot speak English or French at all. Other common languages are Italian, Chinese, German, and Portuguese. Many aboriginal peoples use their own traditional languages. About fifty Indian and Inuit languages are spoken in Canada.

This sign in Schefferville, Quebec, is in **Naskapi, Inuktitut, and English.** Preservation of native languages is important to many of Canada's indigenous peoples.

Religion

Indian and Inuit beliefs honor the forces of nature and worship ancestral spirits. The modern descendants of Canada's earliest inhabitants have blended age-old customs with modern traditions.

However, the number of Canadians who adhere to ancient beliefs is small. Most Canadians follow Christianity. Early French settlers brought the Roman Catholic faith to Canada, and modern Canada is about 42 percent Catholic—the largest single religious group in the country. Another 40 percent of Canadians belong to Protestant sects, predominately the United Church of Canada and the Anglican Church of Canada. Smaller religious communities—including those of the Greek Orthodox, Jewish, Buddhist, Muslim, and Ukrainian Catholic faiths—are scattered throughout the country.

If you'd like to find out more about Canadian cultural life, go to vgsbooks.com, where you'll find links to websites that have information on various cultural customs, food and recipes, holidays and festivals, music, art, literature and more.

Literature

Canadian literature has been influenced by the diversity of the nation's peoples as well as by the diversity of its geography. Many works focus on frontier life or nature, and travel writing has always been an important genre. Since Canada was settled by Europeans, most Canadian literature has been written in French or English. However, since World War II, Canadian literature has begun evolving toward a more distinct voice, with more literature being published in languages other than French or English. Aboriginal writers are also beginning to emerge.

Early French Canadian writers focused on preserving their unique culture in the face of British conquest. Many works celebrated the themes of home and tradition, as in the 1863 novel *Les Anciens Canadiens,* by Philippe-Joseph Aubert de Gaspé. During the 1860s, a group of French Canadian poets called the School of Quebec became prominent. Quebec's first female novelist, Laure Conan, published *Angeline de Montbrun* in 1884.

In English, Frances Brooke published the first Canadian novel, *The History of Emily Montague,* in 1769. Thomas Chandler Haliburton stands out as one of the first authors born in Canada. His 1836 book *The Clockmaker, or Sayings and Doings of Samuel Slick of Slickville* was among the first published Canadian criticisms of Americans. Charles Sangster was an important early English-speaking Canadian poet.

Toward the end of the century, most English-speaking Canadian novelists wrote historical romances. In 1909 Lucy Maud Montgomery published *Anne of Green Gables*, one of the most famous and beloved Canadian novels ever written.

In the first half of the twentieth century, romantic views of rural life continued to be an important theme in literature, as in *Maria Chapdelaine*, by Louis Hémon. But more realistic literature also began to emerge. *Trente Arpents*, by Ringuet, was more critical of the hardships of rural

L. M. Montgomery

life. Other important authors are Gabrielle Roy and Yves Thériault, who wrote powerful novels that describe rural and urban life. After World War II, French Canadian poetry experienced renewed popularity, as poets explored the complexities of the postwar world.

In the 1930s and 1940s, Morely Callaghan and Hugh MacLennan emerged as major literary forces in English. Callaghan authored novels with a spiritual emphasis, and MacLennan explored the tensions between Canada's two main cultures. The writer Robertson Davies gained fame in the 1970s. He sometimes used humor to poke fun at everyday life, both in his novels and in his newspaper columns.

In the modern era, Margaret Atwood has gained tremendous popularity for her novels—such as *The Handmaid's Tale*, which was made into a movie—which focus on women in society. The poet, novelist, and screenwriter Michael Ondaatje, whose most popular books include *The Collected Works of Billy the Kid: Left Handed Poems* and *The English Patient*, is another of Canada's most

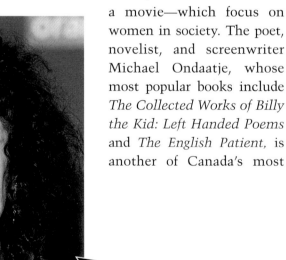

Author Margaret Atwood
is one of Canada's most renowned and award-winning novelists. Her works include *The Blind Assassin*, *Cat's Eye*, and *Surfacing*.

successful writers. Farley Mowat writes about many subjects, and often his books are based on historical events. Carol Shields and W. P. Kinsella are other prominent Canadian writers. Successful Indian authors include Beatrice Culleton, Thomas King, and Tomson Highway.

The Arts

In the twentieth century, the Canadian government began to support the arts as one way to preserve and develop Canada's distinct culture. But creative Canadians have long produced works of artistic importance. Canada's earliest prominent artist was Paul Kane—a nineteenth-century painter who journeyed through western Canada by snowshoe. His artworks depict the lives of the region's Indians. James Wilson Morrice worked in the late 1800s and early 1900s to create memorable Canadian landscape paintings.

After World War I, the Group of Seven (and later the Canadian Group of Painters) developed a style of landscape painting that featured brilliantly colored scenes of wilderness areas. Their works, which were often exhibited together, promoted the arts found in all the country's provinces. Emily Carr was perhaps one of the group's most famous members.

The Montréal painters Jean-Paul Riopelle and Alfred Pellan developed the *automatiste* movement in the late 1940s. This style used a surreal, or dreamlike, technique to represent fantastic or grotesque images that sometimes had a political message.

Sculpture is another important art form practiced in Canada. The Inuit make fine works out of ivory and soapstone. Many of the pieces

CIRQUE DU SOLEIL

The Cirque du Soleil, or "Circus of the Sun," is like no other circus in the world. Hailing from Quebec, the unforgettable production features an all-human cast—there are no animal acts. The striking performance highlights circus arts and street entertainments, featuring wild costumes, magical lighting, and original music.

Cirque du Soleil has its roots in Baie-Saint-Paul, Quebec. In 1982 a group of young street performers came up with the idea of organizing an entertainers' festival. Cirque was launched in 1984 as part of the celebrations surrounding the 450th anniversary of Jacques Cartier's arrival in Canada.

The show debuted in the small Quebec town of Gaspé and was then performed in ten other cities throughout the province. Soon the show spread to the United States and Europe. The cirque even established two permanent theaters in Las Vegas, Nevada, and one at Walt Disney World in Orlando, Florida. In 2001, nearly six million people saw a Cirque du Soleil show.

Created by Marlo Armengol, this statue, titled *Family of Man*, stands in front of the University of Calgary Education Building in Alberta. It was originally displayed at the 1967 World's Fair in Montréal.

depict objects or scenes from ordinary life. Artists in Quebec are famous wood-carvers.

The theater arts are also popular in Canada. Every year a summer festival is held at Stratford, Ontario, where the plays of Shakespeare and other dramatists are presented before large audiences. Another annual event features the plays of George Bernard Shaw. For the French-speaking citizens of Canada, Le Théâtre du Nouveau Monde (the New World Theater) performs in Montréal. Regional drama, opera, and dance troupes also draw enthusiastic crowds.

Popular Culture

Canada's popular culture has transcended the nation's borders, as many popular Canadian performers have gained worldwide fame. Three talented women—Joni Mitchell, Alanis Morissette, and Céline Dion—have had tremendous success as singers. Gordon Lightfoot, Bryan Adams, and Shania Twain are also successful Canadian pop singers.

Founded in 1936, the Canadian Broadcasting Corporation (CBC) is the most

The Canadian government wants to ensure that Canadian musicians have a reasonable chance for success. It requires that at least 35 percent of popular music selections played every week on AM and FM radio stations be Canadian.

Singer and songwriter **Alanis Morissette** was born and grew up in Ottawa. She was involved in theater and television as a child and teenager, before launching her highly successful musical career.

important force in Canadian television. Broadcasting in English, French, and several aboriginal languages, CBC has stations all over the country. It is also a major producer of shows and series. In 1999 Canada launched the Aboriginal Peoples Television Network (APTN), believed to be the world's first public television service for indigenous people.

Canada has an important motion picture industry. The National Film Board of Canada, created in 1939, trains and develops filmmakers and is well known for its award-winning documentaries, short films, and animated films. Thousands of Canadians are employed in the American motion picture industry because many Hollywood films are shot in Canada, where it is less expensive to shoot. Important film festivals are held each year in Vancouver, Toronto, and Montréal. James Cameron, director of the record-setting movie *Titanic*, is a well-known Canadian movie director. Famous Canadian actors include Jim Carrey, Donald Sutherland, Carole Laure, and Graham Greene, an aboriginal actor who starred in *Dances with Wolves*, among many other works.

Food

Canadian cuisine includes dishes from around the world and reflects the diverse populations that that have emigrated to the country from other lands. Chinese immigrants introduced dishes such as Peking duck (slow-roasted duck), while Italian newcomers brought veal scallopini and pasta dishes. Russian influence comes through beef Stroganoff (beef and mushrooms in cream sauce, served with noodles). Swedish pancakes attests to the presence of Scandinavians in Canada. French Canadian diners enjoy favorites such as poutine (french fries

FRENCH TOAST

The sugar maple trees that grow in southeastern Canada produce the delicious maple syrup used in this popular dish.

2 eggs	butter or margarine
¼ cup milk	4 slices of bread
nutmeg or cinnamon (optional)	real maple syrup

1. Break the eggs into a dish wide enough to fit a slice of bread. Beat the eggs lightly with a fork. Add the milk (and a dash of nutmeg or cinnamon if you'd like), and beat some more.
2. Put some butter or margarine in a frying pan and melt it over medium heat. Set one slice of bread in the egg mixture. Flip it so both sides soak up a little egg batter.
3. Cook the soaked bread until it is brown, turning once. Repeat with other slices, adding butter or margarine to pan as needed.
4. Place French toast on a plate and smother it with maple syrup.

smothered in brown gravy and cheese), ratatouille (eggplant casserole), and tourtière (savory meat pie). Historical dishes such as beaver tail, seal flipper pie, and moose roast are still available in many tourist destinations, but most Canadians maintain a varied diet.

◯ Sports and Recreation

Lacrosse—an ancient Indian game—was once Canada's major sport. This competition challenges teams armed with long sticks to scoop up

Although **Mario Lemieux** owns and plays for the NHL's Pittsburgh Penguins, the Montréal-born player skated for the 2002 Canadian Olympic hockey team.

Canadian figure skaters David Pelletier *(back right)* and Jamie Salé *(front right)* display their **Olympic gold medals** with rival Russians, Yelena Berezhneya *(front left)* and Anton Sikharulidze *(back left)*.

a ball, run with it toward the opponent's goal, and fling it into a net. More recently, hockey has by far surpassed lacrosse in popularity and is almost a religion for many people. Professional and amateur hockey teams attract large numbers of fans, and many Canadian children begin to compete when they are seven years old. The biggest Canadian hockey heroes include Wayne Gretzky, Gordie Howe, and Bobby Orr. When the Canadian hockey team beat the United States at the 2002 Olympics, millions of fans thrilled at what has been called one of the most memorable days in Canadian sports history.

Other important sports in Canada are baseball, football, and soccer. In some cases, professional athletes from both Canada and the United States play in the same leagues.

With its widespread national parks system—established in 1885—and its variety of climates, Canada offers its citizens a broad range of recreational activities. Snow skiing and ice skating are common in winter, and swimming, canoeing, and hiking are favorite summer pasttimes.

GOLDEN CONTROVERSY

In addition to Canada's much-celebrated gold medal in hockey, Canadians won several other medals at the 2002 Winter Olympics. These included a controversial gold medal for the figure-skating pair of Jamie Salé and David Pelletier. The controversy began after the Canadians skated a nearly flawless routine that drew cheers from the crowd. During the Russian couple's final skate, the man bobbled the landing on a double axel jump. But the Russian pair was awarded the gold, leaving the Canadians with the silver. The audience booed loudly after the decision, and the media expressed outrage. Four days later, after it was learned that one of the judges may have sold her vote, Olympic officials awarded Salé and Pelletier a second gold medal. The Russians also kept their gold medal.

THE ECONOMY

During the twentieth century, Canada changed from a primarily agricultural producer to a nation that earns its living mainly through services and industry. The nation has remarkable resources for strong economic growth—a variety of minerals and fuels, much farmable land, and natural beauty that attracts millions of tourists each year. For decades, Canada used its huge output of grain and raw materials to purchase goods that it did not produce itself. More recently, manufacturing has expanded and earns more than the agricultural and resource sectors. Yet Canada cannot sell all of its huge manufacturing inventory to its own relatively small population. As a result, the Canadian economy is heavily dependent on foreign trade.

The United States is by far Canada's largest trading partner. Between 1989 (when the FTA went into effect) and 1994 (when NAFTA superseded it), trade between the two countries increased by about 50 percent. Since then, trade has increased by another 40 percent. Trade

agreements work toward reducing trade barriers and tariffs and establishing trade rules. The United States accounts for about 87 percent of Canada's total exports and 67 percent of its total imports.

Other markets important to Canada are in Great Britain, Japan, France, and Germany. Russia and the People's Republic of China have bought large quantities of Canadian wheat. This dependence on world trade makes Canada vulnerable to global trends in prices for its major exports of raw materials.

Services

Services are the largest sector of Canada's economy, employing about 72 percent of the labor force and providing about 67 percent of its gross domestic product (GDP, the value of goods and services produced in a country in a year). Services are especially important in metropolitan areas. Community, business, and personal services make up the largest group of services, a group that includes education, health care, data processing, and legal services. It also includes tourism. About 90 percent of Canada's tourists come from the United States. Tourists are attracted by Canada's national parks, historic cities, winter sports, and annual festivals. One out of ten Canadians makes a living from a tourism-related job.

The second-largest group of service jobs includes finance, insurance, and real estate. Montréal and Toronto are the leading financial cities in Canada. The nation's stock exchange is in Toronto.

Also included in services is transportation. Despite natural barriers that hamper overland travel, Canada has developed an outstanding transportation network. Connecting most parts of the country are railways and highways, supplemented by water linkages.

With about 56,000 miles (90,100 km) of track, Canada's rail system transports about one-third of the nation's freight. Canada's road system includes the Trans-Canada Highway, which runs for 5,000 miles (8,405 km) between British Columbia and Newfoundland. Other long routes head north into the territories. Smaller roadways were built to move people and freight—especially grain—over short distances in the Prairie Provinces. The nation maintains a vast web of water-based linkages, most notably the St. Lawrence Seaway. Built jointly by Canada and the

Canada's **extensive rail system** is one of the main means of transporting freight across the nation's vast countryside.

United States, this waterway helps to bring ships from the Atlantic Ocean to Lake Superior— a distance of more than 2,000 miles (3,200 km). Two airlines— Air Canada and Canadian Airlines—handle most of Canada's domestic and international air traffic. Many parts of northern Canada receive goods, mail, and medical supplies by air. Other important Canadian service industries include government, trade, communication, and utilities.

The Trans-Canada Highway links Newfoundland, on the Atlantic Coast, to British Columbia's Vancouver Island, in the Pacific Ocean. At nearly 5,000 miles (8,405 km), this national highway is the longest in the world. The route includes four ferry rides and a tunnel under the St. Lawrence River.

Industry

The industrial sector—which includes manufacturing, mining, construction, and power—makes up about 30 percent of Canada's GDP. Manufacturing alone accounts for about 18 percent of the GDP. Much of what the country manufactures is based on its own raw materials. Paper (mainly newsprint) and pulp production, for example, depend on the nation's logging industry. Canada is able to refine and sell iron, steel, timber, and petroleum and petroleum-based products. The manufacturing of communications equipment, industrial chemicals, and alcoholic beverages also brings in substantial income.

Among export items, transportation equipment—cars, trucks, aircraft, and subway machinery—ranks high. Processed foods, many of which are based on the nation's livestock and fishing industries, are also important aspects of Canadian manufacturing.

Most of the nation's manufacturing plants are located in the eastern provinces of Quebec and Ontario. Industrial complexes in the Prairie Provinces are connected primarily to the agricultural sector. British Columbia's industries process goods from the region's oil reserves and woodlands. The Atlantic Provinces focus on processing food, iron, steel, pulp, and textile production.

MINING AND ENERGY Canada has a wide range of mineral deposits and therefore a strong mining industry. Mining accounts for about 3.4 percent of Canada's GDP. Most of Canada's minerals come from the Canadian Shield and the western mountains. Potash (used in making fertilizers), iron ore, gold, and uranium exist in abundant quantities. Quebec and Ontario contain large deposits of asbestos (a fire-resistant material), nickel, and copper. In the Cordilleran Region, miners extract substantial amounts of copper, lead, zinc, gold, and silver. Large deposits of coal are found in Nova Scotia and western Canada.

Explorers have discovered extensive oil and natural gas fields in Alberta, British Columbia, and Saskatchewan. These fields supply a substantial portion of the fuel needs of western Canada and parts of the United States. Canada is the world's third-largest producer of natural gas, behind the United States and Russia. In addition, estimates indicate that the 21,000 square miles (54,400 sq. km) of tar sands in northern Alberta contain at least 300 billion barrels of oil—equal in quantity to the world's presently known oil reserves. Sale of petroleum and natural gas accounts for more than 10 percent of the nation's exports, and Canadians themselves consume a large amount of energy per person. This is largely the result of the huge quantities of energy needed to provide heat in severe winters, to transport goods and people across a vast country, and to process natural resources. In addition, Canada's lakes and rivers provide tremendous hydroelectric power.

About 80 percent of Canada's natural gas and oil comes from Alberta, making Alberta one of the richest provinces in Canada. Thousands of miles of pipeline carry the fuels to other parts of Canada as well as to the United States.

Agriculture

At the beginning of the twentieth century, about 65 percent of the Canadian population lived on farms. In modern Canada, only about 23 percent of all Canadians reside in rural areas. Although the number of Canadian farms has declined, improved agricultural machinery, better fertilizers, and stronger seed strains have greatly increased the nation's agricultural productivity. Agriculture accounts for about 2.5 percent of the GDP and employs about 3.6 percent of the labor force.

Many Canadian farmers belong to cooperatives—groups of farms that pool their resources to sell their products at fair prices and to buy needed goods at reduced costs. Wheat, the best-known Canadian field crop, is mainly grown in Manitoba, Saskatchewan, and Alberta. Barley, oats, and flax (a flowering herb whose seeds yield a valuable oil) are among other items produced in western Canada. New Brunswick and Prince Edward Island grow large potato crops. Apples are cultivated in Nova Scotia, New Brunswick, Quebec, Ontario, and British Columbia. Pears, peaches, plums, grapes, and tobacco thrive in southern Ontario.

In addition to growing wheat, western Canadian farmers also raise cattle for markets in eastern Canada and the United States. Pig farms

One of the country's most important crops, **wheat** is grown on farms across western Canada.

are concentrated in Quebec, Ontario, and Alberta. Quebec and Ontario contain most of Canada's dairy farms. Although trappers still bring in pelts from the wilderness, most animals sold for their fur are raised on commercial farms.

Also included in agriculture are forestry and fishing. Canada's vast forests (covering 54 percent of the country's land) are the source of the raw materials for much of its pulp and paper industries. British Columbia supplies almost two-fifths of the nation's timber. Quebec and Ontario also contain considerable wooded areas. Together, these three provinces are responsible for about 80 percent of the nation's annual logging operations. The trees most often cut down are cedar, fir, pine, spruce, and hemlock. About 5 percent of Canada's export sales come from finished wood, and another 5.7 percent come from newsprint and pulp wood.

Logging truck

Loggers have often cut more trees than they have planted. In addition, careless logging practices have left thousands of cut trees to rot. Acid rain and fire have also destroyed huge areas of woodland. The Canadian government has renewed its efforts to protect and renew the nation's forests.

In 2002 lumber producers were facing a stumbling industry. Profits were drying up, mills were closing, employment was falling, and whole communities were losing their economic base.

FISH FARMING

Because the ocean's stock of many kinds of fish is dwindling, Canadians are supplementing the fish supplies through farming. Fish farming is also called aquaculture—the raising of fish, shellfish, or seaweed in a controlled environment. By regulating food, breeding, and water conditions, an aquaculturist can produce large numbers of healthy water life in a short period of time. Aquaculture is particularly successful in Newfoundland and Labrador, where the province's bays and coves are sheltered from harsh Atlantic storms. Fish are kept in tanks or in mesh pens set in coastal waters. Tiny holes in the mesh allow a constant flushing of seawater, so the water in the pen remains fresh and stocked with nutrients.

The biggest reason was a trade dispute with the United States, which is by far the largest importer of Canadian wood. The dispute caused the United States to impose duties and penalties of up to 30 percent on Canadian wood. In addition, a massive infestation of beetles was eating its way through prime trees. Experts have predicted that it could be as long as a decade before the forest industry recovers.

The earliest visitors to Canada noted its fine fishing grounds, especially along Newfoundland's coast. In modern times, the fishing industry continues to be a primary part of Canada's economy, with over one hundred species of fish and shellfish in surrounding waters. Canada exports about three-fourths of its entire annual catch.

The Atlantic coast, with its important ocean currents, supplies large amounts of cod and brings in smaller hauls of herring, sardines, and pollack. Along the Pacific shore, fishers concentrate on salmon fishing, although salmon stocks have fallen due to overfishing. The Canadian government has banned fishing of certain kinds of salmon. The majority of Canada's seafood is canned, frozen, or smoked for export.

◉ The Future

Canada is a huge nation with abundant natural resources. Thanks to NAFTA, foreign trade has been a critical contributor to a stable

Visit vgsbooks.com for up-to-date information about Canada's economy and a converter with the current exchange rate where you can learn how many Canadian dollars are in a U.S. dollar.

economy. Thanks to strong social programs like universal health care, Canadians enjoy one of the world's highest standards of living. Canada has a beautiful and varied landscape, to which even urban dwellers have easy access. In addition, ethnic diversity has given the country a rich and uniquely Canadian personality.

But that personality has shown some cracks, and in the coming years a few important issues must be dealt with. Finding happiness for all of Canada's ethnicities—especially French-speaking and aboriginal peoples—is a major priority. Maintaining a healthy relationship with the United States, while in many ways living in its shadow, is another. If not dealt with gracefully, these issues may become volatile, but they, like biting winters, are key elements of Canada's history and of its future. Tolerance and fairness—as well as strong foreign trade—will be crucial for Canada as it faces the challenge of keeping its national unity intact.

The Canadian flag waves proudly above Banff National Park.

Timeline

CA. 18,000 B.C.	The first humans inhabit Canada.
CA. 3000 B.C.	The first Inuit arrive in Canada.
A.D. 1002	Leif Eriksson probably reaches Baffin Island and the coast of what would become Newfoundland.
1497	Explorer John Cabot lands on the eastern coast of Canada, somewhere between Newfoundland and Nova Scotia. He claims the region for England.
1535	Explorer Jacques Cartier claims the land at two Indian villages for France. The villages would later become Montréal and Quebec City.
1583	Sir Humphrey Gilbert claims Newfoundland for England.
1610	English explorer Henry Hudson discovers the Hudson Bay.
1615	French missionaries arrive in Canada to convert Indians to Christianity.
1627–1632	The British and French fight a war in Europe and North America.
1763	The Treaty of Paris is signed, giving all of France's territories in what later became Canada to the British.
1769	Frances Brooke publishes the first Canadian novel, *The History of Emily Montague*.
1774	The Quebec Act is passed by the British government, giving the French Canadian population religious liberty and the right to follow their own laws.
1784	New Brunswick is established.
1791	The Constitutional Act splits Quebec into the colonies of Upper Canada and Lower Canada.
1837	Revolts take place in Upper and Lower Canada.
1841	The Act of Union joins Upper and Lower Canada, creating the Province of Canada.
1860s	The poets of the School of Quebec become prominent.
1867	The British North America Act forms the Dominion of Canada.
1870–1873	Canada acquires Manitoba, the Northwest Territories, British Columbia, and Prince Edward Island.
1885	Louis Riel leads the North West Rebellion of Métis against the Canadian government.
1898	The Yukon becomes a territory of Canada.
1905	Alberta and Saskatchewan are added to the Dominion of Canada.

1909	Lucy Maud Montgomery publishes *Anne of Green Gables.*
1914-1918	More than 600,000 Canadians serve in World War I.
1931	The Statute of Westminster, establishing Canada's independence, is passed by the British Parliament.
1936	The Canadian Broadcasting Corporation (CBC) is founded.
1939-1945	More than one million Canadians serve in World War II.
1949	Canada becomes a founding member of the North Atlantic Treaty Organization (NATO).
1953	The first year of the Stratford Festival of Canada, in Stratford, Ontario
1962	The Trans-Canada Highway, the nation's first coast-to-coast road, is completed.
1965	The maple leaf becomes the symbol on Canada's first official flag. A national health insurance program is introduced.
1969	The Official Languages Act is passed.
1971	Canada is officially declared a multicultural nation.
1980	Voters in Quebec reject a proposal to separate from Canada.
1982	The Constitution Act is passed.
1989	Canada and the United States sign the Free Trade Agreement (FTA).
1993	Jean Chrétien of the Liberal Party becomes prime minister.
1994	The North American Free Trade Agreement (NAFTA) with the United States and Mexico is established.
1995	Another referendum on secession is held in Quebec, and is defeated by only a 1 percent margin.
1996	*The English Patient,* by Michael Ondaatje, becomes a worldwide hit movie and wins the Oscar Award for Best Picture.
1998	The Supreme Court rules that no province can secede without the consent of the national government.
1999	Nunavut becomes the nation's third territory.
2002	The Haida Indians take the government to court over land rights to the Queen Charlotte Islands.

COUNTRY NAME Canada

AREA 3.8 million square miles (9.8 million sq. km)

MAIN LANDFORMS Appalachian Region, Arctic Archipelago, Canadian Shield, Cordilleran Region, Interior Plains, St. Lawrence Lowlands

HIGHEST POINT Mount Logan, 19,850 feet (6,050 m) above sea level

LOWEST POINT Sea level

MAJOR RIVERS St. Lawrence, Columbia, Mackenzie, Yukon, Nelson, Churchill, Fraser

ANIMALS Beavers, mink, muskrat, moose, deer, bighorn sheep, bears, seals, walrus, caribou, polar bears, ducks, geese, trout, perch, bass, whitefish, pike, salmon, halibut, cod, mackerel, haddock, herring

CAPITAL CITY Ottawa

OTHER MAJOR CITIES Vancouver, Toronto, and Montréal

OFFICIAL LANGUAGES English and French

MONETARY UNIT Canadian dollar. 1 dollar = 100 cents

CANADIAN CURRENCY

The Canadian currency is the dollar, which is broken down into one hundred cents. The Bank of Canada, which started operations on March 11, 1935, is the official bank of the nation and prints the country's legal bank notes. The Bank prints notes in $5-, $10-, $20-, $50-, $100-, and $1,000-denominations and until recently also printed $1 and $2 notes. The $1 note was replaced by a coin in June of 1989, and the $2 note was replaced by a coin in February of 1996. Though the notes are not being printed any longer, they are still legal tender. The Bank of Canada does not design, make, or distribute coins. These tasks are the job of the Royal Canadian Mint, which mints coins in denominations of $2, $1, 50¢, 25¢, 10¢, 5¢, and 1¢.

From 1867—when the Dominion of Canada was formed—until 1965, Canada did not have its own flag. Instead it flew the British flag, known as the Union Jack. On February 15, 1965, after several possibilities were discussed and voted on, the Maple Leaf Flag was adopted as the national flag of Canada. The flag is red and contains in its center a white square bearing a red maple leaf. Red and white are the official colors of Canada, and the maple leaf was historically used to symbolize the land and its people. Maple sap has been an important food source for Canadians since the time of the earliest aboriginals.

Canada's national anthem, "O Canada," was composed in 1880, when Calixa Lavallée, a well-known composer, wrote the music and Sir Adolphe Basile Routhier wrote the French lyrics. The song was first performed at a banquet in Quebec City on June 24 of that year but did not take hold as an official anthem for Canada. Many English versions have appeared over the years, but the version on which the official English lyrics are based was written in 1908 by Justice Robert Stanley Weir. "O Canada" was proclaimed Canada's national anthem on July 1, 1980, one hundred years after it was first sung. The official lyrics are below.

O Canada!
Our home and native land!
True patriot love in all thy sons command.

With glowing hearts we see thee rise,
The True North strong and free!

From far and wide,
O Canada, we stand on guard for thee.

God keep our land glorious and free!
O Canada, we stand on guard for thee.

O Canada, we stand on guard for thee.

For a link where you can listen to Canada's national anthem, "O Canada!" go to vgsbooks.com.

Flag National Anthem

DAN AKROYD (b. 1952) Akroyd is a comedian and screenwriter from Ottawa, Ontario, who began his career in Toronto's Second City comedy troupe. Akroyd gained fame on the television show *Saturday Night Live* and later starred in many films, including *The Blues Brothers* and *Ghostbusters.*

MARGARET ATWOOD (b. 1939) Atwood, from Ottawa, Ontario, is a novelist and poet. She has received high praise for her poetry collection *The Circle Game,* and for novels such as *The Handmaid's Tale* and *The Blind Assassin,* which won the Booker Prize in 2000.

EMILY CARR (1871–1945) One of Canada's most-recognized artists and writers, Emily Carr painted the skies, forests, and native Indian cultures of the Pacific Northwest in a style noted for its intense energy and shimmering light. She was the most famous of the artists known as the Group of Seven. She was born in British Columbia.

JIM CARREY (b. 1962) Born in Newmarket, Ontario, Carrey is one of Canada's most famous actors. His first major film role was *Earth Girls Are Easy,* after which he moved on to the television sketch comedy show *In Living Color.* Since then he has starred in many hit movies, including *Ace Ventura: Pet Detective, Batman Forever, The Truman Show, Liar Liar, Man on the Moon, How The Grinch Stole Christmas,* and *The Majestic.*

JEAN CHRÉTIEN (b. 1934) Canada's prime minister since 1993, Chrétien has been well liked and successful because of a down-to-earth leadership style and years of experience in Parliament. He was born in Shawinigan, Quebec.

ROBERTSON DAVIES (1913–1995) Born in Thamesville, Ontario, Davies was a renowned journalist, playwright, essayist, and novelist. He is best known for his novels, of which he wrote eleven. Nine of them were grouped together as three separate trilogies.

CÉLINE DION (b. 1968) Dion is a popular singer from Charlemagne, Quebec. Dion recorded only in French until 1990. Since then, she has released *Unison, céline dion,* and *The Colour of My Love* in English, becoming a star in both languages. In 1992 Dion won an Oscar Award for the theme song from the movie *Beauty and the Beast,* and in 1998 she won an Oscar for the song "My Heart Will Go On," from the movie *Titanic.*

WAYNE GRETZKY (b. 1961) Born in Brantford, Ontario, Gretzky went on to become a National Hockey League superstar. In twenty years in the NHL he was an eleven-time scoring champion and a nine-time Most Valuable Player. Overall, he holds sixty-one NHL records, including most career points, goals, and assists. Gretzky is considered by many to be the best team sports athlete ever.

TOMSON HIGHWAY (b. 1951) An Indian author from Brochet, Manitoba, Highway writes plays about life on reserves. *The Rez Sisters* and *Dry Lips Oughta Move to Kapuskasing* have won awards and have been staged all across Canada.

E. PAULINE JOHNSON (1861–1913) Also known as Tekahionwake, Johnson moved to British Columbia in 1909. Many of Johnson's poems, such as "The Song My Paddle Sings" and "Legends of Vancouver," celebrate her Indian and Canadian heritage.

JONI MITCHELL (b. 1943) Born in Fort MacLeod, Alberta, Mitchell is one of the most influential singer-songwriters of all time. She is widely credited with blazing a path for women who desire to make meaningful music. She has won several Grammy Awards.

MIKE MYERS (b. 1963) Born in Scarborough, Ontario, Mike Myers first gained fame as a cast member on *Saturday Night Live*. He went on to cowrite and star in such hit films as *Wayne's World, Wayne's World 2, So I Married an Axe Murderer, Austin Powers: International Man of Mystery, Austin Powers: The Spy Who Shagged Me*, and *Austin Powers in Goldmember*.

BILL REID (1920–1998) Reid, a highly influential Haida artist, worked for sixteen years in radio in Toronto and in his native province of British Columbia before becoming a world-renowned sculptor and an expert on Haida mythology. His custom-made jewelry depicting Haida mythological figures and his silk-screen prints are celebrated worldwide, as are his massive sculptures.

JEAN-PAUL RIOPELLE (1923–2002) Riopelle, born in Montréal, was an abstract painter and sculptor widely regarded as the father of Canadian contemporary art. His last major work was "L'Hommage à Rosa Luxemburg (Tribute to Rosa Luxemburg)," a narrative fresco of thirty paintings made using spray paint.

PIERRE TRUDEAU (1919–2000) Born in Montréal, Trudeau became Canada's prime minister in 1968 after only three years in politics. Trudeau captivated Canada with his youthful charisma and strong agenda for liberal issues. In 1984 he won the Nobel Peace Prize.

NEIL YOUNG (b. 1945) Young, a guitarist and singer, recorded with groups such as Buffalo Springfield and Crosby, Stills, Nash, and Young. Young has made many successful solo albums, including *After the Gold Rush* and *Harvest Moon.* He was born in Toronto.

BANFF NATIONAL PARK Located in the Canadian Rockies, Banff National Park is a 2,564-square-miles (6,641-sq.-km) area of protected wilderness. The popular park has more than 1,000 miles (1,600 km) of hiking trails, hot springs, historic sites, and the town of Banff—an active hub for dining, shopping, and lodging—at its center.

BATOCHE NATIONAL HISTORIC SITE Located in the town of Batoche, northeast of Saskatoon in Saskatchewan, this large historical park is the site where the Métis fought their last battle against the Canadian militia in 1885. Displays and battle sites tell the story of the battle.

CN TOWER Located in Toronto's Harbourfront area, the CN Tower is the tallest freestanding structure in the world, at over 1,815 feet (553 m) high. The tower has four observation decks—including the Glass Floor Level and the 360 Revolving Restaurant—as well as many other entertainment options.

MOUNT ROYAL Mount Royal is the best known of eight ancient volcanoes in the heart of Montréal. Homes, offices, and the campuses of McGill University and the Université de Montréal lie on the hill's lower slopes. At the top is a park where visitors can cross-country ski in winter and picnic in summer.

PARLIAMENT BUILDINGS On Parliament Hill in Ottawa, the nation's capital, the Parliament Buildings overlook the Ottawa River. The buildings include the Centre Block, where the Senate and House of Commons meet. It has a detailed stone frieze depicting Canadian history, skillfully carved stone pillars, and beautiful stained glass—all works of nationally renowned artist Eleanor Milne.

ROYAL CANADIAN MOUNTED POLICE "DEPOT" DIVISION The Mounties' only training center is located in Regina, Saskatchewan. A tour of the grounds includes a trip through the Centennial Museum, which reveals the history of the Mounties through exhibits of weaponry, uniforms, and photos.

STANLEY PARK This wilderness park is a 1,000-acre (405-hectare) forest located only blocks from downtown Vancouver, British Columbia. Among the many features of the park are the Vancouver Aquarium Marine Science Center, which has displays and activities on the rain forest and Canadian underwater life, and Prospect Point, which offers striking views of the ocean and many beautiful birds.

STRATFORD This small town in western Ontario hosts the annual Stratford Festival, where the plays of Shakespeare and other dramatists are presented before large audiences. The Stratford Festival has become one of the most renowned theater festivals in the world. The town also has shops, an art gallery, and a history museum.

aboriginals: Indians and the Inuit, the first inhabitants of Canada

agricultural cooperative: an organization of farmers, operating for the benefit of those farmers. Cooperative members share expenses and profits.

archipelago: an expanse of water with many scattered islands

flax: a flowering herb whose seeds yield a valuable oil

Inuit: a native people of Canada who live mainly in the far north and who were formerly known as Eskimos

loyalist: a British colonist in North America who remained loyal to Great Britain during the American Revolutionary War

Métis: Canadians with French and native (usually Cree) heritage. The word *métis* means "mixed" in French.

permafrost: a layer of earth that is permanently frozen

pulp: a substance that is prepared from wood and is used in making paper

referendum: a public vote

reserve: a tract of public land set aside by a government where native people are made to live

separatist: a person who favors independence for a part (such as Quebec) of a political unit (such as Canada)

tundra: a treeless plain that is characteristic of arctic (and subarctic) regions, has a permanently frozen subsoil, and has a vegetation of lichen, mosses, dwarf shrubs, and herbs

Glossary

Selected Bibliography

British Broadcasting Company. *BBC News.* **2002.**
Website: <http://news.bbc.co.uk/> **(May 31, 2002).**
This website is an extensive international news source. It contains political and cultural news, as well as country profiles, and is updated regularly.

Cable News Network. *CNN.com.* **2002.**
Website: <http://www.cnn.com/> **(May 31, 2002).**
This website is a news source on all the world's countries, including political and cultural news. It is updated regularly.

Canada Site. **2002.**
Website: <http://canada.gc.ca/main_e.html> **(July 16, 2002).**
The Canada Site is the primary Internet portal for information on the government of Canada, its programs, services, new initiatives and products, and for information about Canada. The site contains an especially useful section on culture and heritage.

Central Intelligence Agency. "Canada." *The World Factbook 2001.* **2001.**
Website: <http://www.cia.gov/cia/publications/factbook/index.html> **(May 31, 2002).**
This website provides a general profile of Canada, produced by the Central Intelligence Agency. The profile includes brief summaries of the nation's geography, people, government, economy, communications, and transportation.

The Economist. **2002.**
Website: <http://www.economist.com> **(May 31, 2002).**
The website for *The Economist* magazine, this site provides extensive news coverage of the world's economies, including "country briefings" (profiles) of nations. It is updated regularly.

The Europa World Yearbook 2000. **London: Europa Publications Limited, 2000.**
This is an annual publication that covers the recent history, economy, and government of most world countries, as well as providing a wealth of statistics on population, employment, trade, and more. A short directory of offices and organizations is also included.

Federal, Provincial and Territorial Advisory Committee on Population Health. *Toward a Healthy Future: Second Report on the Health of Canadians.* **Ottawa, ON: Health Canada, 1999.**
This detailed, 248-page report summarizes the most current information the committee has on the health of Canadians and invites the reader to consider the implications of these findings for current and future policies, practices, and research.

Ivory, Michael. *The National Geographic Traveler: Canada.* **Washington, D.C. : National Geographic Society, 1999.**
This is an in-depth travel guide on Canada.

Kaufman, Deborah and Christine Swiac, eds. *Fodor's Canada.* **New York: Fodor's Travel Publications, 2001.**
This book is a travel guide that includes in-depth chapters on the culture and sights of major cities and geographical regions.

"PRB 2001 World Population Data Sheet." *Population Reference Bureau (PRB).* 2001.
Website: <http://www.prb.org> (May 31, 2002).
This annual statistics sheet provides an abundance of population, demographic, and health statistics for Canada and almost all countries in the world.

Statistics Canada. 2002.
Website: <http://www.statcan.ca/start.html> (May 31, 2002).
A vast and useful resource, *Statistics Canada* is sponsored by the Canadian government and is the official source for Canadian social and economic statistics. Information is provided from publications, electronic data, the census, surveys, and more.

Turner, Barry, ed. *The Statesman's Yearbook: The Politics, Cultures, and Economics of the World, 2001.* **New York: Macmillan Press, 2000.**
This annual publication provides concise information on Canada's history, climate, government, economy, and culture, including relevant statistics.

U.S. Department of State: Bureau of Public Affairs. "Background Note: Canada." *U.S. Department of State.* 2001.
Website: <http://www.state.gov/r/pa/ei/bgn/2089.htm> (May 31, 2002).
This website provides a general profile of Canada, produced by the U.S. Department of State. The profile includes brief summaries of the nation's geography, people, government and politics, and economy.

Watkins, Mel, ed. *Handbooks to the Modern World: Canada.* **New York: Facts On File, Inc., 1993.**
This collection of informative, largely academic essays on Canada is divided into five parts: The Provinces and Territories of Canada; History; Politics; Economics; and Social Affairs. The essays are written by various experts on different aspects of the nation.

Further Reading and Websites

Attractions Canada.
Website: <http://www.attractionscanada.com/english/mainang.htm>
The purpose of this website is to teach visitors about the many attractions of cultural or educational value the country has to offer, including museums, interpretation centers, historical sites, natural parks, festivals, arts, sports events, and more.

Canadian Broadcasting Company, *CBC.com.*
Website: <http://www.cbc.ca/>
The website for the Canadian Broadcasting Company, the largest media outlet in Canada, *CBC.com* has regularly updated news and links to its television, radio, and local stations. It also has an arts page and a kids page.

Corriveau, Danielle. *The Inuit of Canada.* Minneapolis, MN: Lerner Publications Company, 2002.
This book tells the story of the Inuit, among the first humans to inhabit the land that is now called Canada.

Finley, Carol. *Art of the Far North: Inuit Sculpture, Drawing, and Printmaking.* Minneapolis, MN: Lerner Publications Company, 1998.
This book discusses the art of the far north, including cultural traditions behind the art, how the art was made, the geography and resources of the area, and the lifestyles of the people. It includes maps, photographs, and full-color reproductions of pieces.

Grabowski, John F. *Canada.* San Diego, CA: Lucent Books, Inc., 1998.
This book provides a comprehensive overview of Canada, including its history, geography, and culture.

***Hello Canada* series. Minneapolis, MN: Lerner Publications Company, 1995–1997.**
This thirteen-book series covers the history, economy, and culture of each Canadian province and territory.

Hirschi, Ron. *Salmon.* Minneapolis, MN: Carolrhoda Books, Inc., 2001.
Learn about the life cycle of this amazing fish through colorful photos and fascinating text.

Kirk, Connie A. *The Mohawks of North America.* Minneapolis, MN: Lerner Publications Company, 2002.
This book tells the story of the Mohawks, an Indian nation that has lived in Canada for thousands of years.

Kizilos, Peter. *Quebec: Province Divided.* Minneapolis, MN: Lerner Publications Company, 2000.
This book examines the history of Quebec's ethnic conflict as French-speakers have struggled to preserve their cultural, religious, and ethnic identity in an English-speaking country. It looks at how that struggle has led to the movement to make Quebec an independent country.

McNamee, Kevin A. *The National Parks of Canada.* **Toronto, ON: Key Porter Books, 1994.**
This photo book takes readers on a tour of all thirty-seven of Canada's national parks. In addition to photographer J. A. Kraulis's photos, the book also includes archival photos and maps.

Mercredi, Morningstar. *Fort Chippewyan Homecoming.* **Minneapolis, MN: Lerner Publications Company, 1997.**
Follow twelve-year-old Matthew as he learns about his Chippewyan heritage by spending the summer at Fort Chippewyan in Alberta.

Montgomery, Lucy M. *Anne of Green Gables.* **1909. Reprint, New York: Children's Classics, 1998.**
This is the classic novel about Anne, an eleven-year-old orphan who is sent by mistake to live with a lonely, middle-aged brother and sister on a Prince Edward Island farm.

Raber, Thomas. *Wayne Gretzky.* **Minneapolis, MN: LernerSports, 2000.**
Tells the story of the Canadian Wayne Gretzky, the greatest hockey player of all time.

Robinson, Deborah B. *The Cree of North America.* **Minneapolis, MN: Lerner Publications Company, 2002.**
This book tells the story of the Cree, an Indian nation that has lived in Canada for thousands of years.

Rogers, Barbara Radcliffe and Stillman D. Rogers. *Canada.* **New York: Children's Press, 2000.**
This book provides an introduction to Canada, including its history, geography, government, economy, plants and animals, people, and culture.

Sullivan, George. *All About Hockey.* **New York: G. P. Putnam's Sons, 1998.**
This book is an introduction to the national passion of Canada—hockey. This book provides a fundamental understanding of hockey through chapters on its rules, positions, professional leagues, and the superstars of the sport.

Temko, Florence. *Traditional Crafts of Native North America.* **Minneapolis, MN: Lerner Publications Company, 1996.**
Use a variety of everyday materials to create attractive and functional objects based on the traditions of Native North American peoples.

vgsbooks.com
Website: <http://www.vgsbooks.com>
Visit vgsbooks.com, the homepage of the Visual Geography Series®. You can get linked to all sorts of useful on-line information, including geographical, historical, demographic, cultural, and economic websites. The vgsbooks.com site is a great resource for late-breaking news and statistics.

Index

Captions for photos appearing on cover and chapter openers:

Cover: Located in Alberta's Jasper National Park, Spirit Island sits majestically in Maligne Lake.

pp. 4–5 Niagara Falls is a major landmark that straddles the Canadian-U.S. border.

pp. 8–9 Scenic Gap Lake nestles in the Canadian Rocky Mountains.

pp. 22–23 Explorer Leif Eriksson arrives on the Canadian shore.

pp. 40–41 Two young Inuit mothers have a chat.

pp. 48–49 *Untitled* by painter Jean-Paul Riopelle. During the 1940s, Riopelle cofounded the *automatiste* visual arts movement with Alfred Pellan.

pp. 58–59 A collection of Canadian dollar bills and coins

Photo Acknowledgments
The images in this book are used with the permission of: Michele Burgess, pp. 4–5, 11, 17, 18 (both), 38–39; Presentationmaps.com, pp. 6, 13; Wolfgang Kaehler, pp. 8–9, 19 (top), 20, 40–41, 43 (top); Tourism New Brunswick, p. 10; Don Worrall/Travel Arctic, GNWT, p. 12; Fred Gebhart, pp. 14, 21, 43 (bottom), 50, 54, 60, 63 (bottom); Lyn Hancock, pp. 15, 65; © Carl & Ann Purcell/CORBIS, p. 19 (bottom); North Wind Picture Archives, pp. 22–23; Confederation Life Gallery of Canadian History, pp. 24 (both), 29, 32 (bottom); Library of Congress, p. 26; James Ford Bell Library, University of Minnesota, p. 27; © Musee McCord Museum, p. 30; Archives of ON, S271-1582, p. 31; Saskatchewan Archives Board, p. 32 (top); National Archives of Canada, p. 34; © Bettmann/CORBIS, p. 35; Nunavut Tunngavik Inc., p. 36; Office of the Prime Minister of Canada, p. 37; © John Sylvester, p. 42; © Annie Griffiths Belt/CORBIS, pp. 44–45; © Christopher J. Morris/CORBIS, p. 46; © Reuters NewMedia Inc./CORBIS, pp. 47, 57; © Albright-Knox Art Gallery/CORBIS, pp. 48–49; Prince Edward Island Public Archives and Records Office, 2320/38-1, p. 52 (top); © UPPA/ZUMA Press, pp. 52 (bottom); © 373/Big Pictures/ZUMA Press, 55 (top); © Shelly Castellano/ZUMA press, 56; © Todd Strand/ Independent Picture Service, pp. 58–59, 68; © Maxine Cass, pp. 45 (bottom), 63 (top).

Cover: Lyn Hancock